Life Is What You Bake It is as much about a collection of recipes that makes your mouth water and tugs at your heart with food memories as it is about the chronicles and life lessons of a true comeback kid. Vallery Lomas's life's mantra should be 'Punched down, dough always rises again!'"

—**CARLA HALL**, author of *Carla Hall's Soul Food* and Food Network host and judge

Life Is What You Bake It is at once deeply personal and eminently practical. Vallery weaves together evocative stories about honoring family, overcoming disappointment, and pushing through fear. Her insightful tips and inspired recipes will help to make a champion out of any home baker. On top of that, her wisdom teaches us that baking is about more than creating something delicious; it's a means of grounding oneself, connecting to others, and carrying on a personal legacy."

—**CLAIRE SAFFITZ**, author of *Dessert Person*

Vallery is an inspiration as a baker (have you seen Almost-Ate-the-Plate Carrot Cake?), a writer (you're in for some beautiful storytelling), and also as a human, pursuing her passion for baking and continuing it against seemingly impossible setbacks. We're luckier for it."

—**DEB PERELMAN**, author of *Smitten Kitchen Every Day*

This book could have easily been called *Life Is What You Make It!* Vallery proves that if you can put your mind to it, you can achieve it. From her simple, nostalgic Strawberry Smash to her decadent bananas Foster pancakes, there is a recipe in here for everyone!"

—**KWAME ONWUACHI**, author of *Notes from a Young Black Chef*, James Beard Rising Star Chef, and judge on *Top Chef*

Life Is What You Bake It is not only a collection of recipes but also an empowering book that shows us there's often more possible than we can even imagine. Between the recipes (which are so trustworthy since Vallery writes with lawyerly precision!) and the stunning photography, Vallery's stories paint a picture of what it looks like to walk the walk of living out your dreams."

—**JULIA TURSHEN**, bestselling author of *Simply Julia*, host of *Keep Calm and Cook On* podcast, and founder of Equity at the Table

I don't know what's more inspiring, Vallery's incredible and deeply courageous story or her stunning, crave-worthy recipes. *Life Is What You Bake It* truly has it all: the kinds of stories that make you feel like you're hanging out with a good friend, loads of tips that will help you become a better baker, and of course, baked goods that you'll want to totally devour."

—**MOLLY YEH**, Food Network host and cookbook author

Vallery Lomas comes out on top with this winning collection of cookies, cakes, pies, and more. She brings her trademark zest and enthusiasm to American classics and offers up a chapter of easy-to-master French pastries from her life in Paris. Vallery makes everything doable and easy, no matter what your skill level. I can't wait to bake my way through this delicious collection of recipes!"

—**DAVID LEBOVITZ**, author of *Drinking French* and *My Paris Kitchen*

This is a beautiful, bright, timely book, bringing new life to the baking classics. Reading through it, I felt immediately comforted and uplifted by Vallery's writing, which is warm, engaging, and thoughtful. There's something in the book for everybody, no matter their skill level or confidence."

—**RUBY TANDOH**, food writer and author of *Eat Up!*

While the gorgeous photography and delicious recipes immediately drew me in, Vallery's compelling journey and family history kept me turning the pages. This is my favorite kind of baking book: both a tome of reliable recipes that will become staples in my kitchen and a book to curl up with, reading cover to cover."

—**SARAH KIEFFER**, author of *100 Cookies* and *The Vanilla Bean Blog*

Vallery imbues the heart, soul, and joy of a great baker. Her stories of tenacity will inspire you to bake everything from Grandma Leona's Cornmeal Pancakes to fancy French macarons. She will guide you with her endless charm and beautifully written recipes to bake like a champion."

—**ZOË FRANÇOIS**, author of *Zoë Bakes Cakes* and TV host

Life Is What You Bake It

Life Is What You Bake It

Recipes, stories
& inspiration
to bake your way
to the top

Vallery Lomas

CLARKSON POTTER / PUBLISHERS

NEW YORK

To the best woman I know,
who inspires me to
be the best woman I can be,
my mother, Diane

CONTENTS

Morning Treats

32

Cobblers, Pies & Tarts

134

Cakes

177

En France

Cookies & Bars

Bread

Doughnuts
& Other Fried Things

Cinnamon Rolls, page 229

INTRODUCTION

I quit my job as an attorney to become a baker for one simple reason: I had a burning desire to do something different with my life. I could not continue to give the best hours of my day to a job that I wasn't passionate about. After I won *The Great American Baking Show*, I knew that I had a small window of opportunity to take advantage of my success and turn it into a new career path. Pursuing my foodie dreams while working a full-time job as an attorney felt like an impossible task, and I wanted to give myself a real shot to follow my dream career in food media. Five months after my winning television season had been cancelled, I made a firm decision to take the plunge.

Quitting my job felt like a rash decision, but my journals and therapist can attest otherwise: Baking full-time was something I had wanted for years. In some ways, *I was already doing it.* I spent mornings, nights, and weekends baking for Instagram. But in many ways, I wasn't prepared *at all.* As a government attorney with a limited income, I had no assets, no savings, and many (*many*) student loans.

But what I *did* have was a vision of what my life could be! And I knew the importance of articulating that vision by writing it down and mapping out a path. I often tell myself: If you can't even admit to yourself what your dreams are, how on earth can you translate them from your head to reality?

The path I mapped out included building a network of mentors and connecting with other food media pros. It did *not* include writer's block, devoting significant time and energy to SponCon, and losing my senses of taste and smell temporarily, even though those are obstacles I overcame. Less than a year after quitting my job, I did it: I sold my cookbook proposal and was regularly booking work as a food media freelancer.

The rest is history.

I'm still surprised by my gall to start a food blog during my final year of law school instead of looking for a job. It was 2009, and the recession was in full force. I was filled with angst, but I decided to lean into what made me happy instead of dwelling on what I couldn't control. I knew that baking made me happy, because I would excitedly jump out of bed to activate yeast or bake muffins to share with my classmates. And within days of my first experimental recipes, I started to document the results in a blog. I began my final year of law school in an obsessive baking mode, and I baked something new every day that school year.

I have to admit—if there had been no recession, there would have been no blog. And if there had been no blog, there would have been no @FoodieInNewYork Instagram account seven years later. And if there had been no Instagram account, I wouldn't have been discovered by a casting director for *The Great American Baking Show*. And if I hadn't been on *The Great American Baking Show*, I'd probably be looking up case law while sitting in a cubicle instead of living out the bravest life I dared to dream.

From Louisiana to Los Angeles

Despite my love for all kinds of baked goods, I'm drawn to the soulful flavors that are the hallmarks of my upbringing in southern Louisiana. When people think of Louisiana, they think of revelers downing hand grenades on Bourbon Street or eating a bowl of spicy gumbo. But to me, Louisiana means greeting each passerby, whether friend or stranger, with a warm hello. It means humid April evenings spent on the carport peeling just-boiled crawfish while sipping frozen strawberry daiquiris. And it means gathering pecans on walks home from the school bus stop and snacking on the wild blackberries that grow behind my parents' garage. The Southern climate yields a bountiful harvest of sun-ripened fruit, from berries to citrus. Whether it was Granny Willie Mae serving up a skillet blackberry cobbler for her eight growing sons, the lemon curd I made with lemons from the "Take Some" box on the side of our street, or eating a large pink grapefruit straight from Granny's tree, these were the food staples of my childhood.

The Clay Sisters, Easter Sunday in Indianapolis, circa 1940. From left to right: Leona Marcena (my grandmother), Albia Mae, Dorothy Yvonne, Betty Jean, and Mary Catherine

My mom, older sister Lucy, and me

As cozy as my southern Louisiana upbringing was, I knew there was more of the world I wanted to see, so I moved to Los Angeles for college. I loved living in L.A. and attending the University of Southern California. I'd bike from Santa Monica Boulevard up to Malibu. On weekends, I'd explore California's numerous wine regions, from Napa to San Diego. But after six gloriously sunny years in Los Angeles, I began my final year of law school with a gray cloud overhead. In the summer of 2009, the recession was well underway as I was wrapping up an internship with a prominent law firm. I was also helping my sister Lucy (who soon became my roommate) cope with the unexpected and sudden loss of her beloved fiancé, Stanley.

I had always loved baking, but it was something I did only a few times a year—mostly during the holidays. But I had a box of pumpkin cupcake mix gathering dust in my cupboard, and I figured it would be a fun, easy enough project to raise my sister's spirits. I got out my electric mixer, poured a couple glasses of wine, and turned on Coltrane's "My Favorite Things," letting him serenade us as we scooped, measured, and mixed. When I pulled the pan of perfectly domed, golden-brown cupcakes from the oven, their buttery, spiced-pumpkin aroma filled our apartment. We spooned cream cheese frosting on top of each cupcake, then indulged in their crumbly goodness. For a few intoxicating hours, our worries and cares seemed a little farther away.

In the months that followed, whenever I felt the mounting pressure of finding a job during massive layoffs, or when my sister's spirits were down, I thought back to that afternoon of jazz and cupcakes. I wanted to re-create that feeling, so I invited friends over to bake brownies—our baking efforts mixed with girl talk, while the brownies' velvety interior were punctuated with pockets of melted chocolate. I shredded zucchini and chopped walnuts to make cinnamony loaves to share with classmates (the drudgery of CivPro class was a little more palatable with zucchini bread). The more I baked, the more I wanted to bake.

I replicated the cake-like scones from my favorite coffee shop. I made savory tarts with sautéed mushrooms and sliced potatoes. I even began to explore French pastry by making airy chocolate soufflés, melty *gougères,* and hearty quiche Lorraines—all the classics I had discovered during a semester abroad in Paris. My kitchen became the place where I found balance and calm in the midst of law-school demands and the uncertainty of my future.

With the help of the camera on my flip phone, I started to chronicle my baking adventures on a blog. It was a relief to express myself outside the strict confines of legal writing, while staying in touch with my mom and faraway family.

Instead of looking for a job my final year of law school, I decided to return to France after graduating and taking the bar exam. While in France, I became so enamored by macarons—the colorful ganache-filled sandwich cookies—that when I returned to the States, I decided to make and sell them as a business. I also landed my first real job as an attorney in New York City. I was pulled between two worlds—selling macarons on weekends and defending clients on weekdays. As much as I loved making and selling macarons, I didn't think I had the business savvy to curtail my legal career before it had really gotten started. So, I gave up my macaron business and settled into life as a young attorney. Of course I still found ways to bake and took weekend classes at local culinary schools. I was even interviewed for a part-time job at a cupcake bakery (they didn't hire me; they said I cracked eggs too slowly, even though my batter was "lovely").

My blog, which was now seven years old, had always been a creative outlet for me. Deep down, I knew I wanted to write a cookbook, somehow, someday; but I was afraid to admit that, even to myself. Besides, I was convinced that no one was reading my blog other than my mother. I decided to start an Instagram

Canelés, page 98

account for my baking—that changed everything. I quickly amassed more than just followers; I was also getting attention from casting agents. After a few stale auditions, a casting agent from *The Great American Baking Show* slid into my DMs, asking me if I was a fan of the popular Netflix show *The Great British Bake Off* (um, of course) . . . because they were casting for the American version of it—and they wanted *me.*

On set at Pinewood Studios, filming *The Great American Baking Show* in England, August 2017

Competing on
The Great American Baking Show

The next several weeks were a whirlwind: traveling to Los Angeles for the audition, being chosen as a contestant, and preparing for the competition. A month later, I was on a flight to London for one of the wildest experiences of my life.

Mornings on *The Great American Baking Show* started the same: We met in the lobby before dawn and piled into a bus to get to the studio. After a few weeks, the enormous studio with its sprawling gardens started to feel like home. For a grand entrance, we'd walk as a group over the same bridge that Julie Andrews danced on in *Mary Poppins* and into the tent. We then turned around and did it again. And again. Because this was television, and it's important to have lots of footage and angles to choose from.

Once inside the tent and clad in our matching oatmeal-colored aprons, we got to baking, whether it was to make two dozen sandwich cookies in two hours (cookies may seem simple, but sandwich cookies are a technical feat requiring rolling cookie dough to an even thickness and then achieving the proper ratio of cookie to filling) or creating elaborate gingerbread houses.

Challenges often ended up being equal parts hilarity and calamity as we all struggled to finish the task in the allotted time. For the sandwich-cookie competition (my German Chocolate Sandwich Cookies were filled with chocolate, coconut, and pecans) only two of the six baker-contestants, which by some miracle, included me, actually finished. In the final seconds, my "decorative" fresh coconut finish (I grated it so it was like fluffy white snow) was reduced to something far more rustic: drizzles of chocolate and handfuls of coconut that I threw on top of the cookies, hoping that some would land and stick to a chocolate drizzle. Paul Hollywood loved the cookies and I took a win that day.

I survived cookie week and made it to the finale, which we filmed over two days. By this point, we had been in London filming for more than four weeks, and the sixteen-hour filming days and stress of the competition were taking a toll on me. Owing to a combination of stress and a demanding filming schedule, I had lost nearly 20 pounds. I stopped wearing my favorite lipstick, a fiery red lip stain, by episode 3 (I think I left it in an apron pocket one day, never to be seen again). I looked decidedly shabby—a far cry from the photo of the perky, coiffed,

All smiles, as I made it to *The Great American Baking Show* semifinals: "French Week," September 2017

made-up version of myself that was taken on our first day in the white tent and flashed on the screen next to my technical challenge bakes each week.

This was the finale! The shock of surviving the semifinals had worn off. The slate had been wiped clean, and it was anyone's game. My stomach was in knots all morning, but there was no way I'd let a stomachache keep me from baking my best that day. We filmed our usual opening shots: walking into the tent smiling and looking eager, walking to our stations and putting on our aprons, looking expectantly at the judges and hosts. When Ayesha Curry and Spice Adams shouted in unison, "Bake!," I tried to remain calm while baking faster than I ever had in my life.

The final challenge would determine the champion of *The Great American Baking Show* and involved making a tower of three different desserts in five hours. There are some tests that measure skills, and others that try your endurance. Much like the bar exam, this final challenge measured both. It was years earlier, during the three-day California bar exam, that I realized I had a high-intensity "extra gear" I could activate if needed—and now I needed it! The hours whizzed by. I knew I'd have to dig deep in order to finish. With just minutes left, I had completed all three dishes, but I didn't have time for fancy decoration. A hastily piped squirt of whipped cream with a pecan half was the only decoration that adorned my delectable cheesecakes.

With under a minute left, my desserts were finished, but they weren't all yet placed on the tower, and it was mandatory to have the required number of desserts be presented on the tower for judging. One of the other finalists, Molly, asked if I needed help. She hurried over, and Cindy quickly joined us. The three of us carefully placed each piece of cheesecake on the three-foot display tower along with the other two desserts. When time was called, we all embraced; we had survived something we knew no one else could understand. When we finally let go of one another, I slowly (and rather dramatically) collapsed—an outward expression of how I felt on the inside. I felt a mix of elation, exhaustion, and utter satisfaction at what we had all accomplished. I left everything I had in the tent that day. I baked my heart out.

In that test, I had accomplished what I thought was impossible: I beat nine other talented and passionate home bakers and was declared the champion! I had to keep my win quiet for months until the show's airdate so I wasn't able to shout from the virtual rooftops of Instagram or even tell my friends. Plus, I had taken off five weeks from work, unpaid. I arrived home and returned to work the next day.

One occupational hazard of being an attorney is obsessive thinking about what might go wrong. Although I'm generally optimistic, I'm also prone to spend my time and energy imagining potential catastrophes. This experience (from the time of my audition until when the first episode of *The Great American Baking Show* premiered), was not excluded from these fears. I existed in a bizarre purgatory of keeping the biggest secret I've ever had—that I won the whole show—while still managing to draft appeals and supervise my team of attorneys. My weekends shifted from creating content for Instagram to searching for a literary agent, pitching ideas to journalists, and writing a cookbook proposal. But I soon learned there was something much larger brewing.

I cheered as women shared their stories, and I applauded them. I, too, was one of these women who dealt with harassment.

Less than two weeks after returning home, I found myself aghast while reading a *New York Times* article about the allegations of rampant sexual abuse and power-wielding by the Hollywood Elite. One woman spoke out, and others soon followed. A shift in culture was happening. I applauded as women courageously stood up to demand that we no longer tolerate previously accepted sexual harassment and abuse. I cheered as women shared their stories, and I applauded them. I, too, was one of these women who dealt with harassment.

At the time, I didn't know that my groundbreaking accomplishment would be swept up in the waves of the #MeToo movement, canceled as if it had never happened—collateral damage in the fall of the "pastry-archy."

Cranberry Orange Torte, page 213

Months later the show was to premiere. I was overflowing with joy, and I wanted to share this moment with everyone in the community I'd built during my six years as a New Yorker. Of course, all those people couldn't fit in my studio apartment, so I spent the better part of a week trying to find a location that would seat us and screen the two-hour, primetime television *Great American Baking Show* premiere.

I settled on the 40/40 Club, the Jay-Z owned sports bar with huge plasma TVs and private lounges. There was a hefty drink minimum, so I collected $25 from my friends for two drink tickets, put a deposit on my sister's credit card, and reserved a small private area that looked a lot like an oversized karaoke room. That evening, Ayesha Curry and Spice Adams appeared on-screen, and the two-hour premiere kicked off. I had so many emotions bottled up inside of me with nowhere to put them for so many months; when the premiere aired, it all became real and I could finally breathe. The relief I felt was like turning the valve to "quick release" on a pressure cooker.

Cake week was the first hour. "Looks a bit of a mess, but it tastes divine" was Paul Hollywood's verdict on my version of a naked cake for the week's signature challenge: a lemon chiffon cake with a tangy cranberry filling and classic cream cheese frosting. I couldn't think of anything more exciting than actually baking the items that would be featured in the premiere, so I baked this cake for my friends to let them taste what the judges were critiquing.

Then came the second hour of the premiere: bread week. I showcased my Tiger Doughnuts (page 253) that earned me a Hollywood handshake, got first place for my savory puff pastry breakfast roll, and even impressed myself with a Blackberry Lemon King Cake (page 201), earning me the title of Star Baker, the winning baker for that week's challenges.

My thirty closest friends cheered at every positive comment. They booed at each critique. Watching yourself on television with no control over the final edits is the strangest thing. I felt as though I were floating on a cloud of whipped cream, and I didn't think anything could bring me down. The thing about whipped cream, however, is that it isn't stable. Eventually, it melts.

I took the subway to work the next day, and I had a creeping suspicion that some of my fellow A-train riders were among the 4 million people who watched the premiere the night before. The security guard at my job stopped me as I entered

Summer in the city with my girlfriends (left to right: Sophia, Angela, me, and Zoe)

the building. He squinted his eyes and tilted his head. "Do you know Ayesha Curry?" he asked.

I walked into the main room at my job for a meeting. Everyone stood up and *cheered*. "Star baker!" they exclaimed. I always felt a little iffy about my work as an attorney; graduating at the time of the recession had planted seeds of doubt that could never quite be uprooted. I was never sure if my lawyering was good enough. But there was no question that day: I was proud of what I had accomplished.

Six days later, the night before the next episode was to air, I received a call. It was from an unknown 323 area code (Los Angeles) phone number. It was a producer from the show who said, "Trust me, no one is sorrier than us, but the show is canceled." Allegations had resurfaced about Johnny Iuzzini, one of the show's two judges, and his alleged inappropriate behavior during his days as a pastry chef. My season on *The Great American Baking Show* was abruptly canceled. There was no prize for winning, or even the visibility I thought I had bargained for. My historic achievement as the first Black person to win a full season of any iteration of this successful international franchise suddenly seemed like collateral damage. My victory, like so many accomplishments of Black women who came before me, had been effectively erased.

Torts and Tortes

The legal term for doing something bad and being liable for that bad act is a tort. There's a widely held belief about tort law: "When it comes to liability, if you're gonna hit something, *hit something cheap.*"

This makes a lot of sense when it involves car accidents and insurance coverage. Insurance companies have a way of doing math to determine someone's value, or "lifetime earning potential," and some victims are more costly than others. Naturally, insurance companies preferred *cheap victims*—women and people of color are in this category. After the show was canceled, I couldn't help but think I was seen as a cheap victim. If I weren't a woman—a Black woman—would I have been treated differently?

Punched Down, Dough Always Rises Again

When you first knead dough, it's a glob in a bowl. After a while it rises, only to have its air knocked out of it from being punched down. But that punching down actually enables it to rise a second time. Kneaded dough may appear stagnant, but it doesn't stay down for long.

When I got the call that the show was canceled, it knocked the air right out of my lungs. I didn't have the luxury of wallowing in self-pity just yet. I replaced my disappointment with my lawyer hat—my thinking cap. My head swirled with ideas on how to salvage the season that we had filmed so many months earlier. But I quickly learned that the decision was made, and no one—not the producers or the network execs—were interested in hearing my thoughts on how to celebrate the work and sacrifices of home bakers who had stepped away from careers, infants, and even newlywed spouses.

When I realized this, I was down for the count—a puddle on the floor. But that same high-intensity "extra gear" that had kicked in during the final challenge, and the California bar exam, and at so many other seemingly hopeless times in my life, kicked in again. Just like yeast in bread dough, I started my own chain of reactions.

I emailed my friends, a desperate plea as I tried to make something of the mess that was in front of me. One friend from college put me in touch with her publicist-mentor. Within twenty-four hours, this incredible woman had arranged for multiple news outlets to tune in to the Facebook announcement of my being announced as the winner. And they actually wrote articles for major websites like *People*, *Variety*, and *Deadline*. Those stories led to my being booked on CNN's *Headline News* the very next day, which opened the door for even more press opportunities.

The press coverage had a domino effect. I soon received an outpouring of support from other media that wanted to help promote me as the winner and give me a chance to share my story. *Food & Wine* offered to make a video of me preparing one of the winning dishes—the mille-feuilles with eggnog pastry cream. The Hallmark Channel invited me to Los Angeles to film a segment that showed me making passion fruit macarons, and I ended up cohosting a few episodes of a nationally syndicated show on Fox. I was even invited to present the Outstanding Baker award at the "Oscars of the Food World," the James Beard Awards in Chicago. Just months before, I had felt depleted at the show's cancellation, but here I was now, on television sharing my love of baking with everyone. Each new opportunity breathed life back into me, and I was able to stand tall and be proud of my accomplishments. Like the transformative, metamorphic magic of bread dough, I had been punched down and had risen again.

I am the manifestation of my grandmothers' prayers, and their grandmothers' prayers, as well as all their biggest, boldest, most daring hopes and dreams.

So, as I wrote the recipes for this book, it was impossible not to reflect on these matters while I massaged the butter into the flour to re-create my great-grandma's biscuits (see page 36). It soon became clear to me that I am the manifestation of my grandmothers' prayers, and their grandmothers' prayers, as well as all their biggest, boldest, most daring hopes and dreams. My grandmothers instilled in me a love of family and of baking. But they did so much more. Grandma Willie Mae didn't just teach me how to make her million dollar cake (see page 187) and to frost a three-layered cake. And Grandma Leona taught me much more than how to fry Cornmeal Pancakes (page 54). These women exhibited absolute, unshakable resilience, and it seemed I had acquired that, too. And when I needed to dig deep and find that resilience, it was there. Instead of wallowing in disappointment because *The Great American Baking Show* had been canceled, I refused to let a judge's bad behavior set the trajectory of my life. I had taken the lemons I was given and made something better than lemonade—I made lemon curd.

My grandmothers were born just six years apart—1918 and 1924. Grandma Leona was a high school graduate who lived a city life in Indianapolis, while Granny Willie Mae came from a family of prolific farmers and raised eight sons on a homestead in rural Louisiana. Though they lived in different worlds, they both spent the beginning of their adult lives doing exactly the same thing: earning a living by working for white families. World War II may have liberated white women from their own homes, but for Black women, the war got them out of *white women's* homes. After the war, neither of my grandmothers ever worked as a "domestic" again.

This cookbook is a tribute to them—to all of the women in my family. Their resilience and fortitude paved the way for me to develop my own strengths. At its core, this book is about how I overcame extreme and potentially career-defining disappointments to live out my dreams—and how I continue to overcome internal obstacles of doubt and have learned to believe in myself. The actual process of developing the recipes in this book—as well as the values the women in my family have instilled in me—lends context and importance to the doughnuts, the cakes, the biscuits, the cobblers—it's what matters most. Whether they are baking flops or life's biggest wins, I share these stories with you here.

Olive Oil–Chocolate Chunk Cookies, page 122

How to Use This Book

My family, friends, and colleagues unwittingly served as my recipe testers over a lifetime of baking. This book contains the desserts that disappeared first. The ones that people called the next day, week, month, and even year about, requesting it for their birthday. These are the dishes that people told their friends about.

This collection of recipes and stories has been inspired by my journey from growing up in Louisiana, to being a practicing attorney in Manhattan, and eventually following my passion in food. But more importantly, I share recipes and stories from the people who made me and gave me the blueprint for everything from cake to kindness—my parents and grandparents. Granny Willie Mae with her big heart and green thumb—a petite but mighty woman who raised both produce and children. And Grandma Leona in the Midwest, who led a life with resilience and grace for the more than 100 years she blessed us with.

I believe that life in the kitchen is similar to how we move through the rest of the world—it requires a little bit of planning and courage so that you end up with something delicious. I hope that you bake the recipes in this book. I hope that you discover a new way to make biscuits, or a new favorite peach cobbler recipe.

Be sure to read through the entire recipe, headnote, and ending notes before you start baking. There are tidbits that will provide context, as well as tips for how to successfully prepare the recipe.

 Scan here to see video tutorials for some fundamental baking techniques (see below!). Or visit www.foodieinnewyork.com/tutorials to view me demonstrating them.

—Handling Biscuit Dough (Tips for Your Biscuit Practice, page 39)

—Piping Macarons and Using a Piping Bag (Macarons, page 93)

—Making Meringue (Lighten Up! Making Meringue, page 125)

—Weaving a Lattice Crust (Which Crust for Which Pie? page 175)

—Determining Gluten Development (A Strength Test for Dough, page 232)

—Frying Doughnuts (Fry Doughnuts Like a Pro, page 259)

Here are 5 Bits of Baker's Wisdom!

1. Write it down.

Whether it's the new quantities for a recipe that I've doubled or halved, or my list of goals for the month—writing stuff down keeps me focused and on track. This is especially true for those dreams that are so big they seem impossible without divine intervention. By writing them down and keeping them in view, you will manifest those desires and witness them come to fruition!

2. Move with intention.

You don't need to rush through a recipe, just like you don't have to speed through the streets of Manhattan. But act like you've got a destination, remain focused, and move with intention. Turn on some music, pour a cup of tea, and get to baking.

3. Practice bakes perfect.

Like everything else in life, baking can take a little practice to get it right. Aim high and embrace mistakes! There are no failures in baking—just learning experiences.

4. Trust yourself.

Trust your baking instincts! I often feel my grandmother guiding me in the kitchen, and I can hear her voice as I check to see if a cake layer is baked. Use the cues in the recipes to determine when something has completed cooking—even if the timing doesn't match exactly.

5. Have fun!

Enjoy the process! Try to have fun while you're baking and enjoy the satisfaction of whisking eggs, stirring batter, and rolling out dough—and baking up something you'll enjoy eating and can share with others.

A Baker's Pantry (and Fridge!)

Baking is alchemy. A handful of ingredients combine in different ways to make an exciting world of desserts. Here are some basics to keep in your pantry to satisfy a baking whim at a moment's notice.

FLOUR
All-Purpose Flour
Cake Flour
Bread Flour

DAIRY
Unsalted Butter
Milk
Heavy Cream
Buttermilk
Cream Cheese

LEAVENERS
Eggs
Baking Powder
Baking Soda
Instant Yeast
Active Dry Yeast

SWEETENERS
Granulated Sugar
Light or Dark Brown Sugar
Honey

Corn Syrup
Maple Syrup
Molasses

OIL
Vegetable Oil

CHOCOLATE
Dark Chocolate
Milk Chocolate
White Chocolate
Cocoa Powder

NUTS
Pecans
Almond Flour/ Almond Meal

SPICES
Vanilla
Salt
Cinnamon
Nutmeg
Ginger

Some Tools to Get You Started

Here are some of the tools you'll need for baking the basics!

Set of mixing bowls
Small saucepan
Rubber spatula
Wooden spoon
Whisk

Measuring cups and spoons
Sifter
Rolling pin
Cast-iron skillet

9 by 5-inch loaf pan
8- or 9-inch cake pans
Bundt pan
Pie pan

Baking sheet
Muffin pan
Cooling rack
Microplane

If you're aiming to be a star baker, the items below will help you get there.

Electric mixer
Digital scale
Candy thermometer
Skimmer/spider

Food processor
Springform pan
Soufflé dish
Tart pan with removable bottom

Madeleine pan
Copper canelé molds
Piping bag and tips
Large offset spatula

Pastry brush
Pizza slicer
Waffle maker
Rolling pin rings

MORNING

TREATS

What gets you out of bed in the morning? Is it the smell of buttery biscuits (see page 36) wafting through the house? Maybe it's the thought of trying a new recipe for a Raspberry Coffee Cake (page 46) or an oven-baked pancake (see page 57). Whether you want to make homemade English Muffins (page 42) with Strawberry Jam (page 41) or French toast made with banana bread (see page 66), I guarantee you won't be hitting the snooze button on these recipes!

Great-Grandma Lillie's Biscuit Legacy

My dad grew up eating his weight in biscuits slathered with homemade preserves. He spent afternoons taking his red wagon out to the family's orchard, where he'd climb pear trees and shake the branches to loosen the fruit. He'd take his bounty of tree-ripened fruit home to his mother, who'd make preserves.

My dad's grandmother, Lillie, stopped by their Prairieville, Louisiana, home every Sunday when she left church. "I'ma cook y'all some biscuits!," she'd croon. Lillie was a professional cook, and she had worked in restaurants in Texas for more than a decade, starting around World War II. She saved money to move back to Louisiana and bought a house in Baton Rouge. Though her relatives were prolific farmers, she preferred the city.

She'd make a batch of biscuits and serve them to her eight adolescent grandsons. "Y'all eat all you want," she'd say before asking, "Y'all want some more?"

"Yeah!" the chorus of brothers sang.

She'd make up more biscuit dough and keep baking. They ate heartily, piling preserved blackberries and figs on the biscuits, washing it down with cold milk made from milk powder and water pumped from the backyard well, served over ice. "Mmm-mmm! Y'all sure can eat a lot!" their grandmother observed.

Growing up Black and cash poor in rural Louisiana, many resources were limited. Biscuits, however, were not. My great-great-great grandmother Mary, who arrived in Louisiana on a slave ship from Santo Domingo, Hispaniola, and her husband, James Weams, passed down 100 acres of farmland from the Homestead Act. It was replete with an orchard of 50 plum trees and just about every other fruit that flourishes in the subtropical Louisiana climate.

Granny Willie Mae still lives on this land—though it's down to just a few fig and grapefruit trees. I watched her bake her favorite recipes in the same kitchen where Great-Grandma Lillie spoiled my dad and uncles with her bottomless biscuits. This is my modern take on her biscuits.

Willie Mae Dukes Johnson and Lillie Vallery Williams (my grandmother and great-grandmother "Aunt Lillie") and me, Baton Rouge, Louisiana, 1988

Accordion Biscuits

MAKES 1 DOZEN BISCUITS

Biscuit making is in my blood. It's my inheritance—a birthright. But whether or not your lineage includes biscuit makers, I assure you that you can learn to make them too. Proper technique is most important (see my best biscuit-making tips on page 39). Biscuit making is a practice—something to be mastered over time and through experience, rather than a recipe to be memorized. A gentle touch is necessary for a tender biscuit. The quicker you work, the colder your ingredients will remain, and the lighter your biscuits will be. Buttermilk is most often used, but I like a mix of heavy cream and cream cheese for a rich, crumbly biscuit. And I don't knead the dough—I flatten it, cut in half, and stack the two halves on top of each other. This process of flattening and stacking the dough creates layers that rise in the oven like a stretched-out accordion.

4 cups (500g) **all-purpose flour**, plus extra for shaping

2 tablespoons (20g) **baking powder**

¼ cup (50g) **granulated sugar**

2 teaspoons **kosher salt**

1 cup (2 sticks/226g) cold, **unsalted butter**, cut into ½-inch pieces

2 large **eggs**

1⅓ cups (320ml) **heavy cream**

½ (8-ounce) package (½ cup/113g) **full-fat softened cream cheese** or **full-fat Greek yogurt**

Demerara or **granulated sugar**, for sprinkling on top (optional)

make ahead The biscuits can be made ahead through step 6 and then frozen. Continue with step 7, then bake completely frozen for 25 to 28 minutes.

1. Preheat the oven to 400°F and place a rack in the middle of the oven. Line 2 baking sheets with parchment paper and set aside.

2. Whisk the flour, baking powder, granulated sugar, and salt together in a large bowl.

3. Add the butter to the flour mixture and toss to coat each piece with the flour mixture (this will prevent the butter from clumping together). Use your fingertips to smash each piece of butter flat. If any flattened bits are larger than a quarter, break them up, continuing to coat each butter piece with the flour mixture.

4. Set the bowl in the freezer for 5 minutes. Whisk one of the eggs in a medium bowl. Add the cream and cream cheese and whisk to combine.

5. Remove the flour mixture from the freezer and pour the egg mixture over it. Use a large silicone spatula to fold the mixture until the dry ingredients are just moistened. Tip the shaggy dough out of the bowl and onto a floured surface (it's okay if there are some dry bits of flour that aren't yet incorporated).

6. Using floured hands, pat the mixture into an 8 by 6-inch rectangle. Cut the block in half crosswise, and stack one half on top of the other half. Then, repeat the procedure, patting, cutting, and stacking two more times. Pat the dough down one last time until it's 1 inch thick. Using a 2½-inch round cutter, press straight down into the dough without twisting. Repeat, leaving enough space between each round of dough so that the edges don't pinch together. Transfer the rounds to the prepared baking sheets, leaving 2 inches of space between each round of dough. Lightly knead the scraps and repeat to stamp out the remaining biscuits. Place the baking sheets with the biscuits in the freezer for 10 minutes.

7. Meanwhile, whisk the remaining egg in a small bowl. Remove the biscuits from the freezer and brush the tops with the beaten egg. You want the biscuits to be as cold as possible when going in the oven, so work quickly. Sprinkle with demerara sugar, if using.

8. Transfer a baking sheet to the oven and bake until the biscuits have puffed up and are browned on top, 20 to 24 minutes. Remove the biscuits from the oven and repeat with the second baking sheet (or bake both at once if your oven rack allows). Place the baking sheets on a rack to cool slightly before serving.

---

storage The biscuits are excellent warm, but they can be stored in an airtight container at room temperature for up to 3 days, once cooled. The baked biscuits may also be frozen for up to 2 months.

Tips for Your Biscuit Practice

Grandma Willie Mae kept an empty mason jar next to the sink for collecting fat rendered from pork. She used this fat when she made biscuits, and much like vegetable shortening, it stays solid even during the hottest summer days in Louisiana. I have to be honest—I don't cook bacon all that much (and I think butter makes for a tastier biscuit). But, you can still get those luscious layers by following these tips.

1. **KEEP EVERYTHING COLD.** You want the butter in the dough to be cold when you place the biscuits in the oven. If your butter isn't cold enough, the biscuits will be short and dense. All the butter that should have melted and steamed *in* the biscuit dough to create flaky layers will instead be in a puddle beneath the biscuits. It will have melted too quickly and the layers won't pop open.

    If your mixing bowl is still warm from the dishwasher, stick it in the fridge before you start. You can even freeze your flour before you get started (this is really helpful in the hot summer months). The biscuit game is all about doing whatever it takes to keep the butter cold.

2. **WORK QUICKLY.** By working quickly, your ingredients will remain cold. If you tend to work slowly, stick your ingredients and tools in the fridge or freezer in between the steps to keep them chilled.

3. **USE A HOT OVEN.** Okay, I know I just said to keep everything cold—except for the oven! Be sure the oven has preheated completely. There should be a blast of heat when you place the biscuits in. That blast of heat hits the cold butter, and as the butter melts it creates the steam—that's how you get those layers.

4. **HAVE A LIGHT HAND.** Making biscuits is a tactile thing, and you'll master it more easily when you embrace biscuit dough as shaggy with chunks of butter. There's perfection in the imperfection. Biscuit dough is not smooth like a cake batter or cookie dough. Use a light touch and don't overwork the dough.

5. **MAKE CLEAN CUTS.** When stamping out the biscuits, push straight down on the cutter and don't twist it. Twisting seals the layers closed, making for a stout biscuit. Pushing straight down preserves the layers that you've worked so hard to form so your biscuits will rise higher than a stretched-out accordion.

See page 27 for video tutorial instructions on handling biscuit dough.

Strawberry Smash

SERVES 1

Every April, my family piled into my dad's white Mercedes and drove east to Cousin Jateaux's farm to pick the juiciest, ripest strawberries. I rolled my window down to let the warm air whip my face as zydeco and honky-tonk blues played on the radio. The sweet sounds of the harmonica and accordion serenaded us as we drove down Airline Highway. We exited just feet before my dad's hometown of Prairieville, in the much tinier town of Galvez.

My dad greeted Cousin Jateaux, a fair-skinned man with a thick accent who had acquired farmland in addition to the land he inherited from our common ancestors. He gave me a wide, shallow box, and while my mom and older sister sat contentedly in the car, far from the irritating bugs and sticky air, I headed out with my dad into the fields to get to work. Crouching down between the rows of berries growing near the ground was an easy feat for my five-year-old legs and gymnastics-trained core. My tiny hands were the perfect size to pluck only the reddish, plumpest berries that looked as though they would surely burst with sweet juices.

Time whizzed by, and we stayed until Dad and I had filled boxes and boxes of berries, which we ushered into pint-size containers made of windowpane green plastic. At home, my parents boiled the mason jars and mashed berries in our giant gumbo pots, stirring in sugar by the heapfuls for batches of strawberry preserves. My dad always rinsed off some strawberries, plucked the green leafy top off, and placed the berries in a bowl with a sprinkle of sugar for me. He used a fork and mashed 'em up. There was no better reward for a hard day's work, and Strawberry Smash remains my favorite breakfast during strawberry season.

1 cup (140g) extra-ripe fresh strawberries, rinsed and hulled

1 teaspoon granulated sugar

---

1. Place the strawberries in a small bowl and sprinkle the sugar on top.

2. Use a fork to mash the berries with the sugar. This can be enjoyed in the same bowl as it was made in, which is perfect for slurping up the tangy, sweet strawberry juice that collects at the bottom of the bowl.

---

note Supermarket strawberries are grown to be hardy so they can withstand the bumps and bruises of transport without releasing their juices—an excellent metaphor for life itself, but not what you want for this dish. If using supermarket berries, you will need a little more effort to smash the berries with a fork.

My dad and I on our way to Cousin Jateaux's strawberry farm in Galvez, Louisiana, circa 1990

Strawberry Jam

MAKES 4 TO 5 PINTS

Traditions are passed on, and I have finally moved up from the kids' table of "smashed fresh strawberry eater" to the adult work of "strawberry jam maker." Making jam requires a sterile environment—jars, bands, and lids are washed with hot soapy water, dried, and placed on a clean countertop or dish towel before filling with hot jam. I love my parents' technique of flipping the jars over once they are filled with jam and the lids and bands are secured, eliminating the need to process the jars in a water bath. When properly sealed, the center of the lid will be depressed—this lets you know that the jam will not spoil in storage. When you open the jar, weeks or months later, the vacuum seal will pop open, with jam ready to be enjoyed.

3 pounds (about 2 pints) **fresh ripe strawberries**, rinsed and hulled

1 (1.75-ounce) box **powdered fruit pectin** (such as Sure-Jell)

½ teaspoon **unsalted butter**

7 cups (1.4kg) **granulated sugar**

1. Thoroughly wash 5 pint-size (16-ounce) jars in hot, soapy water. Rinse well. Place the lids, bands, and jars in a large pot and submerge in hot water. Bring the water to a boil and simmer for 10 minutes. Turn off the heat and leave in the hot water until ready to fill.

2. Place the strawberries in a food processor and process until they have partially broken down (you can also place them in a large bowl and mash them). You don't want whole berries, but you want to keep a little texture, so don't puree them completely.

3. Transfer 5 cups of the mashed strawberries to a large pot. Stir in the pectin, and add the butter. Cook over medium-high heat, stirring constantly, until the berries reach a rolling boil. This will take some time, so be patient (a rolling boil means that it is boiling aggressively, even when stirred). Add the sugar and stir constantly until it returns to a rolling boil. Continue to stir and cook for 60 seconds, then remove from the heat and skim any foam off the top.

4. Use tongs to remove the jars, lids, and bands from the hot water and place on a clean dish towel. Ladle the jam into the prepared jars, leaving 1 inch of headspace. Place the lids on top of the jars and screw on the bands as tightly as you can. Wipe around the tops of the jars, then check again to make sure they are securely closed. Turn the jars upside down on top of a clean kitchen towel and let sit at room temperature overnight. As the jam cools, the lids will seal. Check that the center of each lid is depressed.

storage The jars of jam can be stored at room temperature, unopened, for 1 year. After opening, refrigerate the jam for up to 1 month.

note You can reuse mason jars, but the lids and bands must be new. Thick rubber gloves and tongs are helpful for handling the hot jars and lids. Do not reduce the amount of sugar in the mixture—it's necessary for the preservation of the jam.

English Muffins

MAKES 1 DOZEN MUFFINS

English muffins are not actually *muffins*. In fact, they aren't even baked! They're a yeast-raised bread that's cooked low and slow on a hot griddle, yielding a toasty exterior with an airy and soft center. Their texture makes them an ideal vehicle for breakfast favorites, from eggs Benedict to butter and jam. Using a cast-iron griddle or skillet helps them bake evenly, since cast iron is ideal for heat distribution. A little patience ensures an even bake—cooked in the middle and beautifully browned on the outside. I enjoy these with butter and jam, or a thick slice of fried green tomato.

4½ cups (560g) **all-purpose flour**, plus extra for shaping

1½ cups (360ml) **milk**, any type

3 tablespoons (42g) **unsalted butter**, melted (just warmer than room temperature, otherwise you could kill the yeast)

4 teaspoons (16g) **granulated sugar**

1 (¼-ounce/7g) package **instant yeast**

1 teaspoon **kosher salt**

Vegetable oil, for the bowl and skillet

3 tablespoons (24g) **cornmeal**, any type

---

1. In the bowl of a stand mixer fitted with the dough hook, add the flour, milk, melted butter, sugar, yeast, and salt. Turn the mixer on to low and mix until all the ingredients are combined. Increase the speed to medium and knead until the dough is smooth, soft, and elastic, about 8 minutes. Use a rubber spatula to scrape the dough into an oiled bowl. Cover the bowl with plastic wrap and let the dough rise until puffed, about 2 hours. The dough won't quite double in size, and that's okay.

2. Once the dough has risen, tip it out onto a floured work surface and divide it into 12 equal pieces. Roll each piece into a ball, then flatten to make a 3½-inch disk. Sprinkle the cornmeal in an even layer on 2 baking sheets, and place the flattened disks on the cornmeal to keep them from sticking to the baking sheets. Cover with a dish towel and let the dough rest for an additional 30 minutes.

3. When the dough is almost finished resting, heat a cast-iron griddle or skillet over medium heat (if you've got multiple skillets, feel free to use them all at once so you can cook as many muffins at the same time as possible).

4. Lightly grease the skillet with a little vegetable oil and reduce the heat to low. Use a spatula to carefully transfer each round of dough to the skillet (be careful not to poke the rounds and deflate the dough). Cook over low heat until lightly browned, 8 to 10 minutes. Flip over and cook the other side until lightly browned, an additional 8 to 10 minutes. (I like to check after about 8 minutes to make sure they aren't cooking too fast. If they are dark brown or starting to burn, reduce the heat to the lowest setting.) Lightly grease the skillet again and repeat with remaining muffins.

5. Test a muffin by slicing it in half—it should be cooked through. If it isn't, lower the heat for the next batch and cook longer to ensure that they are cooked through. (Finish off any undercooked muffins in a 350°F oven for 5 minutes.) Slice in half and enjoy.

storage Cooked English muffins freeze excellently. I slice them in half before freezing, then toast to rewarm.

make ahead You can make the dough through step 2 and let it rest in the refrigerator overnight. The next morning, let it come to room temperature for 20 minutes before continuing to step 3.

Blackberry Oatmeal Cake

MAKES ONE 8-INCH CAKE

This breakfast "cake" uses 3 cups of rolled oats instead of flour. I enjoy making this at the beginning of the week—which is as close to meal prep as I get! It's warm and comforting from the spices, fruit, and nuts, and it's filling in the best way from the fiber-licious oats (and happens to be gluten-free!). Smear your favorite yogurt on a piece if you'd like some faux frosting on top.

Nonstick baking spray with flour

3 cups (270g) old-fashioned rolled oats

1 tablespoon (8g) ground cinnamon

2 teaspoons baking powder

¼ teaspoon kosher salt

6 tablespoons (85g) melted unsalted butter, coconut oil, or vegetable oil

1 cup (240ml) milk, water, or nondairy alternative, like soy or oat milk

¼ cup (50g) packed light or dark brown sugar

¼ cup (80g) raspberry or strawberry jam

2 large eggs

1 teaspoon vanilla extract

1 cup (140g) fresh blackberries or blueberries (see Note)

½ cup (60g) chopped toasted pecans (optional)

1. Preheat the oven to 350°F and place a rack in the middle of the oven. Spray an 8- or 9-inch square baking pan with baking spray and set aside.

2. In a large bowl, combine the oats, cinnamon, baking powder, and salt.

3. In a medium bowl, add the melted butter, milk, brown sugar, jam, and eggs. Whisk to combine.

4. Pour the liquid ingredients into the dry ingredients and stir until combined. Stir in the blackberries and pecans, if using.

5. Pour the batter into the prepared baking pan and spread evenly. Bake until the center of the cake is set and browned along the edges, 35 to 40 minutes. Enjoy warm or at room temperature.

storage The cake can be stored in the fridge in an airtight container for up to 4 days. To reheat, zap it in the microwave, or reheat in a 350°F oven until warm, about 5 minutes.

note You can use any fruit in this dish. If using a larger fruit, like strawberries or apples, chop them roughly before adding them to the batter. You can also skip the fruit altogether!

Raspberry Coffee Cake

MAKES ONE 8-INCH CAKE

The amount of flavor in this cake far exceeds the amount of effort it takes to prepare. The cake batter comes together in minutes, with no electric mixer required. The raspberries do more than add punchy flavor—the soft, juicy berries contrast with the crunchy streusel. I never baked with raspberries before moving to California. Raspberries don't grow in southern Louisiana, so we didn't eat them. But when I moved to Los Angeles, part of my education included getting to know the local produce, and I came to appreciate raspberries for baking.

My first SoCal farmers' market experience was at The Grove. I wandered the covered market, marveling at the luscious fruits, perfectly uniform and lined up in rows, though I was bewildered by the expensive prices (they matched the West L.A. real estate the produce occupied!). This was the Cali version of what we Louisianans simply call "the vegetable stand." I picked up a shiny, perfect-looking half pint of raspberries and have baked with the bright red, semi-tart fruit ever since.

All the things that make a baked good delectable are in this coffee cake: tart raspberries, almondy cake, and crunchy-nutty streusel. This combination makes the cake something you will crave—it will linger in your memory long after it has lingered on your tongue.

---

make ahead The almond streusel can be refrigerated in an airtight container for up to 1 week.

---

note Whenever you're melting butter, cut it into small pieces so it will melt quickly and evenly.

ALMOND STREUSEL

⅓ cup (40g) all-purpose flour

½ cup (50g) almond flour

¼ cup (50g) granulated sugar

½ teaspoon kosher salt

4 tablespoons (½ stick/55g) unsalted butter, melted

RASPBERRY CAKE

Nonstick baking spray with flour

2 large eggs

⅔ cup (160g) sour cream or plain full-fat Greek yogurt

1 teaspoon almond extract

⅔ cup (130g) granulated sugar

1 cup (125g) all-purpose flour

¼ cup (25g) almond flour

1¼ teaspoons baking powder

¼ teaspoon baking soda

¼ teaspoon kosher salt

1¼ cups (170g) fresh raspberries, rinsed and dried

---

1. Prepare the almond streusel: Combine the flours, sugar, and salt in a small bowl. Whisk to combine. Pour in the melted butter. Use a fork to gently stir until clumps form. If there are any clumps that are larger than a chickpea, gently break them up. Store in the refrigerator (so the butter can firm up) while preparing the cake.

2. Prepare the raspberry cake: Preheat the oven to 350°F and place a rack in the middle

RECIPE CONTINUES

of the oven. Assemble an 8-inch springform pan and spray the bottom and sides with baking spray.

3. In a large bowl, combine the eggs with the sour cream and almond extract. Whisk until combined, about 1 minute. The mixture will resemble pale yellow yogurt.

4. Add the sugar, flours, baking powder, baking soda, and salt. Whisk until it comes together in a thick batter, 1 to 2 minutes. Transfer the batter to the prepared springform pan. Place the raspberries in an even layer on top of the cake batter. Sprinkle the streusel on top.

5. Bake until the streusel is starting to brown and the center is set (it won't jiggle when shaken) and a toothpick or cake tester stuck deep into the center comes out clean, 45 to 55 minutes.

6. Remove the cake from the oven and set the pan on a cooling rack for at least 20 minutes, then unmold and slice. Enjoy with coffee or tea for a brunch treat that will impress your friends.

How to Wash Raspberries

Raspberries are so delicate that running them under a faucet can damage them. To rinse them, place them in a colander, then place the colander in a large bowl of water and gently shake the colander. Remove the colander from the the bowl of water and use a salad spinner to dry the berries, or allow them to drip-dry in the colander.

Banana Pecan Bread

MAKES ONE 9 BY 5-INCH LOAF

Banana bread is the perfect comfort-food baking project. It's easy as mash, mix, and bake, yet it manages to distract us from the worrisome things, so we can enjoy the refuge of mindfulness and delicious gratification that baking so readily offers. My banana bread is hearty from the toasted pecans and whole wheat flour. It's not overly sweet, and it has just the right amount of tang from the buttermilk and orange zest. It's also loaded with bananas, which gives you maximum banana flavor *and* moistness. Just don't skimp on the cinnamon, nutmeg, or vanilla—the spices are what take this banana bread over the top.

---

note Once your bananas are super ripe and covered with large dark spots, you can refrigerate them, which will delay further ripening (this will also make their outer peels and inner fruit dark and mushy, but that's just fine for baking).

Nonstick baking spray with flour

½ cup (60g) roughly chopped **pecans**

¾ cup (90g) **all-purpose flour**

¾ cup (90g) **whole wheat flour**

1 tablespoon (12g) **baking powder**

1 teaspoon **kosher salt**

1 teaspoon **ground cinnamon**

½ teaspoon **baking soda**

¼ teaspoon **ground nutmeg**

4 ripe medium **bananas**, peeled

2 large **eggs**

1 cup (200g) packed **light** or **dark brown sugar**

6 tablespoons (85g) **unsalted butter**, melted

½ cup (120ml) **buttermilk** (see page 51)

2 teaspoons **vanilla extract**

Zest from 1 **orange**

---

1. Spray a 9 by 5-inch loaf pan with baking spray. Preheat the oven to 350°F and place a rack in the middle of the oven.

2. Place the pecans in a single layer on a baking sheet and toast in the oven until they take on some color and their aroma fills your kitchen, about 7 minutes. Set the toasted pecans aside. Keep the oven on while preparing the batter.

3. In a medium bowl, whisk together the flours, baking powder, salt, cinnamon, baking soda, and nutmeg.

4. Add the bananas to a small bowl and mash with a fork. In a separate large bowl, whisk

RECIPE CONTINUES

49

the eggs until foamy. Add the brown sugar to the eggs and whisk until it is mostly smooth (if there are any large lumps of brown sugar, use the back of a spoon to break them up). Whisk in the melted butter, buttermilk, and vanilla until combined.

5. Add the mashed banana and dry ingredients to the egg mixture and stir with a spoon or spatula until combined. The batter will be very thick. Stir in the toasted pecans and orange zest.

6. Pour the batter into the prepared loaf pan and smooth the top. Bake until a crust forms on the loaf and a toothpick inserted into the center comes out clean, 50 to 60 minutes.

7. Remove the pan from the oven and set it on a wire rack to cool for 10 minutes, then remove it from the pan and let it cool completely before slicing and serving.

---

storage Store in an airtight container in the refrigerator for up to 1 week or at room temperature for up to 4 days.

Make Your Own Buttermilk

Buttermilk tenderizes baked goods, adds tang, and activates baking soda as a leavening agent. I love to bake with it, but I don't keep it on hand. I prefer to make my own on an as-needed basis, and you can, too.

To make 1 cup of buttermilk, combine a scant cup of milk with 1 tablespoon of distilled white vinegar or lemon juice. Let it sit for 5 minutes so the milk can curdle. You can also substitute sour milk (even if it's curdled) with buttermilk in an even swap.

Pumpkin Bread

MAKES ONE 9 BY 5-INCH LOAF

For all the gloriously sunny days in Los Angeles, it actually gets cold at night due to the desert climate. On those chilly nights, I'd routinely bake pumpkin bread—and it's those kinds of nights that also remind me of studying for the bar exam.

While cramming the rules of evidence into my already saturated brain, I came to realize that the test is passed in the preparation—not during the three days when it's actually administered. When I felt like no other mnemonics for memorizing the components for burglary would fit into my head, I'd fix myself some green tea and bake this mix-and-bake pumpkin bread, giving my racing brain a break.

While studying for the bar, I learned how to train my mind to not let anything hold me back—even if a question stumped me. Though I might not have an idea what the answer was, I had to try to answer it anyway. I soon discovered that I had that high-intensity "extra gear" I could shift into when I needed an extra boost of energy. The aroma of this bread always reminds me that I can shift gears to overcome anything, whether it's a bar exam, a soupy crème caramel made during a baking competition, or a disappointing show cancellation that seemed insurmountable. The pressure just pushes me to be even better!

Nonstick baking spray with flour

1⅔ cups (200g) all-purpose flour

1 teaspoon baking soda

½ teaspoon baking powder

1½ teaspoons ground cinnamon

¾ teaspoon ground nutmeg

1 teaspoon kosher salt

1 cup (200g) granulated sugar

½ cup (120ml) vegetable oil

2 large eggs

1 teaspoon vanilla extract

1 cup (240g) pumpkin puree

¼ cup (60ml) buttermilk (see page 51)

1. Spray a 9 by 5-inch loaf pan with baking spray. Preheat the oven to 350°F and place a rack in the middle of the oven.

2. Add the flour, baking soda, baking powder, cinnamon, nutmeg, and salt to a large bowl and whisk to combine.

3. In another large bowl, whisk together the sugar and oil. Add the eggs and vanilla and whisk until the mixture is thick and yellow, 1 to 2 minutes. Add the pumpkin puree and mix until creamy and orange, 1 to 2 minutes. Finally, whisk in the buttermilk until combined.

4. Use a rubber spatula to fold the wet ingredients into the dry ingredients until no streaks of flour remain. Pour the thick batter into the prepared loaf pan and smooth the top with the back of a spoon or spatula. Bake until your kitchen is filled with the aroma of pumpkin spice, a crust forms on the loaf, and a cake tester inserted into the center comes out clean, about 55 to 60 minutes.

5. Remove the loaf from the oven and let it cool on a wire rack for 10 minutes, then remove it from the pan and let it cool completely before slicing and serving.

storage The cake stores in an airtight container for up to 5 days.

Moist Muffins and Loaves

Quick breads and muffins are excellent treats for novice and advanced bakers alike. No tools are needed other than a bowl, spoon, and can-do attitude (though a rubber spatula and a whisk are helpful). Everything comes together easily because the fat is in liquid form (melted butter or vegetable oil); all you need to do is fold the wet ingredients into the dry until just combined.

The biggest threat to making moist quick breads is under- or over-baking. Don't be fooled by the delicious aroma of the bread wafting through your kitchen—it might not yet be baked through. To test for doneness, insert a cake tester into the deepest part of the loaf, usually the center. I like to use a thin wooden skewer, since a toothpick isn't long enough for most loaves. Pull out the cake tester— you don't want to see any crumbs clinging to it. This will ensure that your loaf is baked all the way through. The Banana Pecan Bread (page 49) and the Pumpkin Bread (opposite) can also be baked in a muffin tin. Since muffins are smaller, they'll bake much more quickly than loaves.

Cornmeal Pancakes

MAKES 15 PANCAKES

I spent summers with Grandma Leona in my mom's hometown of Indianapolis. It was there I learned that steamed rice with a little butter and sugar is as good a breakfast as cheesy grits. A true Midwesterner, Grandma Leona didn't eat grits—but she *had* grit. The fourth of ten children, Grandma was prone to Depression-era cooking strategies.

She always added a little milk to eggs before scrambling them, "to make them stretch," she'd tell me as I eyed her with a mix of curiosity and suspicion. Why eggs needed to be "stretched" was beyond my seven-year-old comprehension; however, I now appreciate Grandma's resourcefulness, as well as the fluffiness of eggs whisked with a little milk before scrambling.

The most popular dish in Grandma's repertoire showcased her innovation with food: she would fry leftover cornbread batter into these cornmeal pancakes as she hummed hymns and moseyed about her red kitchen. This tasty hybrid of cornbread and pancake was the perfect way to make another meal from leftover cornbread batter, but eventually she started making these whether or not there was leftover batter from the day before.

The pancakes have some grit from the cornmeal and crisp edges from the oil they're cooked in. Grandma would use her giant cast-iron skillet, whose heavy bottom ensured that the pancake cooked evenly and all the way through. But a griddle or other skillet will give those results, too. The baking powder gets to work as soon as the wet ingredients are mixed with the dry, so whip up the batter just before you're ready to get cooking. A pat of butter and some maple syrup are all these pancakes need, and the Cranberry-Maple Syrup (page 276) pairs with them beautifully.

¾ cup (90g) **all-purpose flour**

½ cup (70g) finely ground **yellow cornmeal**

3 tablespoons (35g) **granulated sugar**

1 teaspoon **baking powder**

½ teaspoon **kosher salt**

½ teaspoon **baking soda**

¼ teaspoon **ground nutmeg**

2 large **eggs**

1½ cups (360ml) **buttermilk** (see page 51)

3 tablespoons (42g) **unsalted butter,** melted

Butter or **vegetable oil,** for the skillet

Maple syrup or **Cranberry-Maple Syrup** (page 276)

Leona Marcena Clay Johnson at age 98, November 2016

RECIPE CONTINUES

1. In a large bowl, combine the flour, cornmeal, sugar, baking powder, salt, baking soda, and nutmeg.

2. In a medium bowl, whisk the eggs with the buttermilk and melted butter until combined.

3. Pour the wet ingredients into the flour mixture and stir until just combined. Don't overmix—the mixture will be lumpy, as pancake batters should be.

4. Heat a griddle or large skillet over medium heat. Once the surface is hot (a drop of water will dance across the pan), add 2 teaspoons of butter or oil and swirl to coat the pan. Once the oil is sizzling hot, use a ¼-cup measure to scoop the batter onto the hot skillet. You should hear the skillet sizzle as the batter hits it. Continue to add the batter, leaving enough space between the pancakes so they can be easily flipped. Cook until bubbles cover the top of the pancakes and break open, about 2 minutes. Flip the pancakes over and cook until the other side is golden as well, an additional 1 to 2 minutes. Repeat until all the pancakes are made. Serve warm with maple syrup or the Cranberry-Maple Syrup.

Bananas Foster Oven-Baked Pancake

SERVES 4 TO 6

At the end of my first year of law school, I went to New Orleans for the summer to work at a legal nonprofit. The workload was heavy, so I always welcomed having a lunch break with my colleagues. We would venture over to Canal Street for the best deal in town, a "Temperature Lunch" at the Palace Café, where the cost of a prix fixe menu reflected whatever the temperature was that day. Was it 96 degrees? That's $9.60, please.

The food was great, but the dessert was the best. Legend has it that bananas Foster was born at this very place, so of course I always ordered that. Our server cooked the brown sugar in butter tableside and sliced the bananas right into the molten sugar so they could lightly caramelize, before dousing them with high-proof rum and lighting the mix on fire. The flambéed bananas were served with a scoop of vanilla ice cream because when it's 96 degrees out, you need something to cool you down, especially with those flames.

Now I make bananas Foster as a topping for this oven-baked pancake that comes together in a blender and can rest up to 12 hours before baking. When you're ready to bake, pour the batter into a cast-iron skillet that's sizzling with hot butter. This pancake rises beautifully in the oven, much like a soufflé, billowing up into an airy, crispy-exterior delight. And if you add ice cream, this makes a perfect dessert.

OVEN-BAKED PANCAKE

½ cup (60g) **all-purpose flour**

2 tablespoons (30g) **granulated sugar**

½ teaspoon **kosher salt**

3 large **eggs**

½ cup (120ml) **milk,** any type

1 teaspoon **vanilla extract**

4 tablespoons (57g) **unsalted butter**

BANANAS FOSTER TOPPING

4 tablespoons (57g) **unsalted butter**

¼ cup (50g) packed **light** or **dark brown sugar**

2 medium **bananas,** peeled and halved lengthwise

1 teaspoon **ground cinnamon**

3 tablespoons (45ml) **light** or **dark rum**

---

1. Prepare the oven-baked pancake: Combine the flour, granulated sugar, salt, eggs, milk, and vanilla in a blender. Blend on medium until the mixture is homogeneous, about 30 seconds. If there's any flour clinging to the sides or bottom of the blender, use a spatula to scrape it down and blend for an additional 10 to 15 seconds. Transfer the batter to the refrigerator to rest for up to 12 hours.

2. When you're ready to bake the pancake, preheat the oven to 400°F and place a rack in the middle of the oven.

RECIPE CONTINUES

3. Place the butter in a 12-inch cast-iron skillet and heat in the oven for 5 minutes. This will melt and brown the butter. Remove the skillet from the oven and carefully swirl the butter around to coat the sides of the skillet. Be careful not to spill the butter, since it's hot.

4. Gently stir the pancake batter. Pour the pancake batter into the center of the skillet and carefully return the skillet to the oven. Bake until the pancake is puffed in the center and browned around the edges, 20 to 25 minutes.

5. Once the pancake has been in the oven for 10 minutes, prepare the bananas Foster topping (it's important that the topping is ready at the same time the pancake is ready so that the bananas Foster sauce doesn't separate). Melt the butter in a medium skillet over medium-low heat. Add the brown sugar and stir with a wooden spoon until dissolved, 1 to 2 minutes. The mixture may appear separated, and that's okay. Add the banana slices and sauté on each side until golden, 2 to 3 minutes per side. Remove from the heat. Sprinkle the cinnamon on top, then add the rum. Return to medium-low heat and stir until the mixture comes together and thickens slightly, another minute or so. Remove from the heat.

6. Once the pancake is golden brown and puffed, stir the topping until the bananas are well coated and the sauce is blended. Remove the pancake from the oven. Spoon some of the sauce from the topping over it, then place the sliced bananas on top. Slice and serve straight from the pan, spooning more sauce over each serving.

Crispy-Ridged Buttermilk Pancakes

MAKES 1 DOZEN PANCAKES

The best part of pancakes is the crispy brown ring that forms around the edges when they're cooked in a hot griddle with sizzling oil. My mom always adds a little almond extract to the pancake batter—whether she's making homemade or using a box mix—which adds a distinct nutty flavor. These pancakes are also fluffy, light, and tangy from the buttermilk.

1⅓ cups (160g) all-purpose flour

1 teaspoon baking powder

1 teaspoon baking soda

1¼ cups (300ml) buttermilk (see page 51)

¼ cup (50g) granulated sugar

2 large eggs

2 tablespoons (28g) unsalted butter, melted

1 teaspoon kosher salt

¼ teaspoon almond extract

Vegetable oil, coconut oil, shortening, or butter

Smoking Points

Vegetable oil has a higher smoke point than butter. If you cook the pancakes in butter, you'll need to wipe the skillet after every few pancakes, since butter has milk solids that burn. But if you want the buttery taste with the crispy edges, use clarified butter (like ghee), which has a much higher smoke point because the milk solids have been removed.

1. Combine the flour, baking powder, and baking soda in a large bowl and whisk together.

2. Whisk the buttermilk, sugar, eggs, melted butter, salt, and almond extract together in a medium bowl until thoroughly combined.

3. Pour the liquid mixture over the dry mixture and whisk until no large pockets of flour remain. (It's okay if there are some tiny lumps.)

4. Heat a large skillet over medium-low heat. Once the surface is hot (a drop of water will dance across the pan), add 2 teaspoons of oil and swirl to coat the pan. Once the oil is sizzling hot, use a ¼-cup measure to scoop the batter into the hot skillet. You should hear the skillet sizzle as the batter hits it. Leave enough space between the pancakes so they can easily be flipped. Cook until bubbles cover the top of the pancakes and break open, about 2 minutes. Flip the pancakes over and cook until the other side is golden as well, an additional 1 to 2 minutes.

5. Remove the pancakes from the skillet and add more oil before cooking the next batch. Repeat until all the pancakes are made. Serve warm.

note By scooping the batter into the skillet using a measuring cup, you ensure that the pancakes are all the same size.

Sweet Potato Pecan Waffles

MAKES 10 WAFFLES

When you have a large family, one sure sign of how delicious something is will be how quickly it disappears. The first time I made these waffles, they disappeared so fast that there was no evidence they ever existed. Their pillowy texture is thanks to egg whites whipped to stiff peaks. I wouldn't ask you to whip and fold egg whites before noon unless it's really worth it—and these waffles are *definitely* worth it!

2 cups (500g) mashed cooked **sweet potatoes** (2 to 3 large sweet potatoes; see page 155)

1 cup (240ml) **milk**, any type

2 large **eggs**, separated, plus 4 **egg whites**

¼ cup (50g) packed **light** or **dark brown sugar**

4 tablespoons (55g) **unsalted butter**, melted

1¾ cups (210g) **all-purpose flour**

1 tablespoon (10g) **baking powder**

2 teaspoons **ground cinnamon**

½ teaspoon **ground ginger**

½ teaspoon **kosher salt**

¼ teaspoon **ground nutmeg**

Melted butter or nonstick cooking spray, for greasing the waffle iron

1 cup (120g) **pecans**, toasted and chopped (optional)

1. Combine the smashed sweet potatoes, milk, egg yolks, brown sugar, and melted butter in a large bowl. Use a fork or whisk to blend until the mixture comes together. (It's okay if there are a few stubborn bits of sweet potato.)

2. Add the flour, baking powder, cinnamon, ginger, salt, and nutmeg. Stir until it comes together; the mixture will be paste-like, heavy, and dense.

3. In another large bowl, use an electric mixer on medium speed to whip the egg whites until stiff peaks form, about 3 minutes. Use a rubber spatula to stir one-third of the whites into the batter to lighten it. Once the egg whites are incorporated, fold in the remaining two-thirds until no streaks of the egg whites remain, about 30 seconds.

4. Heat a waffle iron. When ready, coat the iron with a little butter, oil, or cooking spray. Pour about ½ cup of the batter into the center of the iron and sprinkle 1 or 2 tablespoons of the pecans (if using) on top. Close the lid and cook according to the manufacturer's directions, until the waffle is cooked through and golden brown. Repeat until all the waffles are cooked. Serve warm.

Waffle Swirl

MAKES 5 WAFFLES

Two flavors of batter are swirled together to make these fluffy waffles with spirals of chocolate and vanilla in each bite. They are the perfect reminder that chocolate and vanilla—and all the flavors and colors in between—belong together on one plate.

On those mornings when you can't be bothered making waffles from scratch, there's no shame in pulling out the box mix. Prepare the batter according to the package directions and divide it in half. Add the melted chocolate to one half of the batter, then proceed to step 5. These waffles are delicious as is, but you can top with maple syrup, freshly whipped cream (see page 274), or fresh berries.

1⅔ cups (200g) **all-purpose flour**

¼ cup (50g) **granulated sugar**

1 tablespoon (12g) **baking powder**

½ teaspoon **kosher salt**

2 large **eggs**

1¼ cups (300ml) **milk**, any kind

6 tablespoons (85g) **unsalted butter**, melted

½ teaspoon **vanilla extract**

2 ounces **unsweetened** or **semisweet dark chocolate** (see Note), melted

Melted butter, **oil**, or **nonstick cooking spray**

1. Add the flour, sugar, baking powder, and salt to a large bowl and whisk to combine.

2. In a medium bowl, combine the eggs and milk and whisk to combine.

3. Drizzle the milk mixture into the flour mixture, whisking until combined. Then add the melted butter and vanilla and whisk until well combined.

4. Equally divide the waffle batter into 2 bowls. In one bowl, add the melted chocolate and whisk to combine.

5. Heat a waffle iron. When ready, coat the iron with a little butter, oil, or cooking spray. Dollop ¼ cup of batter from each bowl into the waffle iron and swirl using a butter knife (the batter will start to set as soon as it hits the hot iron). Close the top and cook according to the manufacturer's instructions. Remove when done and continue to make the waffles, coating the iron's surface when necessary. Serve warm.

---

note Unsweetened chocolate will yield the most dramatic and colorful swirls, but semisweet dark chocolate also works beautifully.

French Toast

MAKES 8 PIECES

French toast was the first thing I cooked for myself after *The Great American Baking Show* was abruptly pulled off air. Wallowing in disappointment, I had no desire to eat—let alone bake. But as I transferred the milk-and-egg-soaked stale bread to a hot skillet, I couldn't help but feel hopeful. I figured, *If old, dry bread could be revived and transformed into something delicious from a little milk and eggs on a hot griddle, surely I could be revived, too.* The act of making French toast lifted my spirits, and I knew things could still be delicious if I mixed in some creativity and stretched my imagination and resources.

French toast is a dish where creativity gets you bonus points. Brioche and challah breads are both made from a dough enriched with eggs and milk, so soaking these breads in the custard and cooking the slices on a griddle make a divinely rich French toast. But that isn't where the opportunities end: you can French-toast some banana bread, pound cake, wheat sandwich slices—in fact, you can French-toast just about anything. Serve with butter, confectioners' sugar, or maple syrup, or see the suggestions that follow.

---

3 large **eggs**

¾ cup (180ml) **milk**, any kind

1 tablespoon (12g) **granulated sugar**

1 teaspoon **vanilla extract**

1 teaspoon **ground cinnamon**

½ teaspoon **kosher salt**

8 (1-inch-thick) slices **bread of choice** (see pages 231, 241)

Butter or **oil**, for the griddle or pan

1. In a medium bowl, whisk together the eggs, milk, sugar, vanilla, cinnamon, and salt. Drench the bread slices in the egg mixture one at a time until each is soaked, about 1 minute per side.

2. Heat a griddle or large skillet over medium-low heat. Once the surface of the griddle is hot (a drop of water will dance across the pan), add 2 teaspoons of butter or oil and swirl to coat the pan.

3. When the oil is sizzling hot, add a coated bread slice or two to the griddle, leaving space between them. You should hear the sizzle. Cook until golden brown, about 3 minutes, then flip the slices to cook on the other side until golden brown, another 3 minutes. Remove and continue to make the French toast, adding a little butter or oil to the griddle as needed. Serve warm.

SERVING SUGGESTIONS FOR FRENCH TOAST

Berries and Pound Cake: This decadent twist on French toast is fantastic on its own, but serving with Vanilla Whipped Cream (page 274) and fresh berries adds a light touch.

Gone Bananas!: For a doubly banana French toast, top French-toasted Banana Pecan Bread (page 49) with the bananas Foster topping (see page 57), whipped cream (see page 274), sliced fresh bananas, and toasted pecans.

Nutty Pumpkin Bread: Cozy up by topping French-toasted Pumpkin Bread (page 52) with whipped cream (see page 274), cream cheese frosting (see page 187), and a sprinkle of toasted nuts.

Tangy Berry Twist: Top French-toasted challah or brioche with Maple Vanilla Butter (page 273), Lemon Curd (page 278), maple syrup, and smashed fresh blackberries.

EN
FRANCE

Food can mirror the best parts of our humanity in transcending individual cultures, languages, and expectations. When I was a college student living in Paris, I discovered delicate pastries that tasted as beautiful as they looked. I became fluent in French and I developed my philosophy on life: we may speak different languages, practice different religions, and have different ethnic backgrounds, but we have common hopes and dreams.

The French pastries weren't as sweet as the Southern desserts I grew up eating (the tarts were indeed *tart*!). But the sparkles of light racing up and down the Eiffel Tower each night satiated my soul in a way that only a dream realized can. I spent weekends and breaks traveling to nearby European and African countries—I was living my wildest dreams. And France taught me to dream even bigger and to savor each moment, salty or sweet.

My First
Taste of France

My Francophilia and obsession with French pastry has tropical origins. When I was fifteen, I spent three weeks one summer grooving to the melodic patterns of Zouk music in Guadeloupe, a French Caribbean island. Cindy, an exchange student who had stayed with my family in Louisiana the summer before, invited me to her home the following summer. I cashed in $900 of savings bonds that were gifts from my godmother from the past nine Christmases to buy my plane ticket, and off I went to eat mangoes so sweet they left a layer of juicy, sugary film on the tip of my nose, my cheeks, and my chin. It was my first trip out of the country, and it was my first taste of French culture outside of Louisiana.

I was welcomed there with a Creole feast of colombo (goat stew) and boiled plantains. We said our bonjours and au revoirs paired with the classic French greeting, *la bise* (the kiss-kiss on both cheeks). These were Black Caribbeans—descendants of African slaves who pledged allegiance to the tricolor, hacked up their "*r's*" in the back of their throats when they said *garçon*, and seamlessly transitioned their conversations from Creole to textbook French.

Cindy's mother packed us a picnic of papayas, guavas, and almond croissants for a hike to Les Chutes du Carbet, a glorious waterfall. The yeasty Viennoiserie were buttery and delicious, but there were no layers that shattered when you bit into them since the hot and humid island temperatures didn't allow the butter to stay cold enough for lamination. We devoured the juicy tropical fruits and delicious pastries after a hike through the forest, wading in waist-deep water through various small rivers. This was the kind of experience that can happen only once—my first taste of both almond croissants and being immersed in a culture completely different from my own. It was the start of both my Francophilia and my love of travel.

Clafoutis

MAKES ONE 10-INCH CAKE

My first French *gâteau* was not from a fancy *pâtisserie*—it was a homemade clafoutis by my French host mother. Here was a barely sweet, single layer cake, studded with cherries and so eggy it flirted with crossing into flan category. The crispy, near-caramelized almondy edges and custardy center challenged my previous conceptions of what exactly "cake" could be. You can serve this warm; I like it best the day it's made, but you can also refrigerate the leftovers. They make an excellent breakfast with a cup of coffee. As a variation, you can substitute 12 ounces of fresh raspberries for the cherries.

Softened **unsalted butter,** for the baking dish

¾ cup (150g) **granulated sugar,** plus
2 tablespoons for the baking dish

5 large **eggs**

1 cup (240ml) **whole milk**

1 cup (240ml) **heavy cream**

1 teaspoon **kosher salt**

1 teaspoon **vanilla extract**

2 teaspoons **kirsch** or **brandy** (optional)

¾ cup (90g) **all-purpose flour**

Scant 1 cup (90g) **almond flour**

12 ounces **cherries,** stemmed and pitted (see Note) if fresh, or defrosted and drained if frozen

Confectioners' sugar

1. Preheat the oven to 350°F and place a rack in the middle of the oven. Smear a 10-inch round gratin dish with some softened butter to coat the inside. Sprinkle 2 tablespoons of granulated sugar into the dish and rotate the dish so that the sugar coats the bottom and sides (much like a soufflé, the batter uses the sugar like rungs of a ladder to climb the side of the dish).

2. Combine the eggs, the remaining ¾ cup sugar, the milk, cream, salt, vanilla, kirsch (if using), and flours in a large bowl or a blender. Whisk or blend until smooth and lump-free.

3. Pour the batter into the prepared baking dish. Arrange the cherries on top. Bake until the batter starts to pull away from the fruit, there are cracks across the top, and the top starts to brown, 45 to 55 minutes. While baking, the batter will creep up the sides of the dish and eventually rise nearly 2 inches over the top of the dish. The edges will brown before the center does.

4. Set aside to cool for 10 minutes; the risen clafoutis will deflate. Sprinkle with confectioners' sugar just before serving.

note My host mother said that the traditional method is to leave the cherry pits in for flavor. This is one tradition I'm fine breaking; however, if you choose to leave the cherry pits in, be sure to give a heads-up to those you share the dish with.

Twice-Baked Almond Croissants

MAKES 4 CROISSANTS

I'm pretty sure my Guadeloupean adventure when I was a teenager contributed to my insatiable appetite for traveling and exploring new places. My favorite way to relive that feeling of wonder and excitement is to re-create the delicious pastries I tried there, like these almond croissants. The pastries embody a waste-not attitude, as bakeries use day-old croissants. They're actually baked twice—once when they're first made and again after they've been slathered inside and out with almond cream. Since you don't actually need to make croissants yourself to make these, this is a simple way to transport a bit of France to your kitchen. They are best the day they're made, either warm, straight from the oven, or at room temperature.

4 plain **croissants**

4 tablespoons (55g) **unsalted butter,** room temperature

¼ cup (50g) **granulated sugar**

½ cup (50g) **almond flour** or **almond meal**

1 large **egg**

1 tablespoon **all-purpose flour**

¼ teaspoon **almond extract** (optional)

2 tablespoons **sliced almonds**

Confectioners' sugar

1. Preheat the oven to 350°F and place a rack in the middle. Line a baking sheet with parchment paper.

2. Use a serrated knife to cut each croissant in half lengthwise, like a sandwich. Set the croissants aside.

3. Add the softened butter and granulated sugar to a large bowl. Use a rubber spatula to mix until it's creamed, about 1 minute.

4. Add the almond flour, egg, all-purpose flour, and almond extract (if using). Continue to mix until well combined.

5. Smear about 1½ tablespoons of the almond cream into the center of the bottom half of each croissant, and use the back of a spoon or a butter knife to smear the cream into an even layer from tip to tip.

6. Set the top of the croissant on top and smear a tablespoon of almond cream on it as well. Sprinkle one-fourth of the sliced almonds on top of each croissant and transfer the croissants to the prepared baking sheet.

7. Bake until the cream on the outside appears cooked and lightly browned, 15 to 20 minutes. Transfer to a cooling rack. Sprinkle with confectioners' sugar and serve.

VARIATION

No-Bake Cream-Filled Croissants
Use a serrated knife to cut 4 croissants in half lengthwise, like a sandwich. Add ¼ cup of "cheat" vanilla pastry cream (see page 277; you'll need 1 cup total) to the center of the bottom half of each croissant, and use the back of a spoon, butter knife, or small spatula to smear the cream into an even layer from tip to tip. Set the top of the croissant on top. Dip the tops of the croissants into a shallow bowl of Creamy Vanilla Glaze (page 276), sprinkle with desired toppings (such as rainbow sprinkles or mini chocolate chips), and set aside on a plate or rack for a few minutes for the icing to set before serving.

Crêpes

MAKES 1½ DOZEN CRÊPES

The Paris I grew to love was cold, damp, moody, and smoky. On rainy days (which were often), I left my apartment to head for what I always now crave when it rains—crêpes. In Paris, crêpes are street food, griddled while you wait, folded hot into a triangle for you to hold so the warmth from the pancake also warms your frigid hands.

"*Bonjour, monsieur! Une crêpe beurre-sucre, s'il vous plaît,*" I purred in my best French. He ladled the thin batter onto the round *billig*, then picked up the T-shaped squeegee-like tool and quickly and adeptly spread the puddle of batter into an even, round circle in one lyrical movement. I patiently watched as the batter set. He then ran a giant, thin metal spatula under the crêpe, and flipped it over, placing a pat of butter on top. The butter bubbled and danced before giving way to the heat and disappearing into the thin pancake. The final act was a sprinkle of sugar before it was expertly folded into a giant triangle, slipped into a sleeve, and passed finally into my hands. The warmth from the crêpe extended from the palms of my hands to my core.

My crêpes may be a little smaller than the ones I had in Paris, but they are just as light, warming, and satisfying. Serve them with a small pat of butter, sprinkle of sugar, and squirt of lemon juice. They are also excellent served with Nutella and topped with sliced bananas or strawberries.

make ahead The crêpe batter can be prepared the day before.

1⅓ cups (160g) **cake flour**

3 tablespoons (45g) **granulated sugar**, plus extra for serving

4 large **eggs**

2 cups (480ml) **whole milk**

4 tablespoons (55g) **unsalted butter**, melted, plus extra melted butter for the pan

2 teaspoons grated **orange zest**

Dash of **kosher salt**

2 tablespoons (30ml) **orange liqueur**, **rum**, or **orange juice** (optional)

---

1. Combine the cake flour, sugar, eggs, milk, melted butter, orange zest, salt, and orange liqueur (if using) in a blender on low speed for 10 seconds. Increase the speed to medium for 10 seconds, then stop the blender and use a spatula to scrape down the sides and bottom. Blend on medium speed an additional 10 seconds. Let the batter rest, covered, at room temperature for 1 hour or in the refrigerator for up to 24 hours.

2. Heat a 9- or 10-inch nonstick skillet over medium-low heat. When the skillet is hot, brush it lightly with melted butter. (You'll know the skillet is hot enough because the butter will sizzle and dance around the skillet.)

3. Measure a scant ¼ cup of batter in the center of the skillet. Pick up the skillet by the handle and swirl in a circular motion so that the batter coats the bottom in an even layer, avoiding hitting the sides of the skillet (the batter will start to set immediately, so swirl

RECIPE CONTINUES

quickly). It's okay if there are a few spots that the batter doesn't get to before it sets—just leave it be.

4. Cook until the crêpe starts to brown around the edges and the bottom side is set, about 90 seconds. Use a spatula to loosen the edges, following the circumference of the crêpe. Then, carefully slide the spatula under the crêpe and flip. (If you're having a hard time flipping, let the crêpe cook a little longer.) It's okay if the crêpe folds on itself as you flip—just straighten it out.

5. Cook on the other side until the crêpe is golden, about 60 seconds. Shake the skillet back and forth, then slide the crêpe out of the skillet onto a plate. Keep cooking and stacking, one crêpe on top of the next, adding more butter to the pan as needed. Continue until all the crêpes are cooked. (If you notice the crêpes getting darker and crisper as you cook, turn the heat down a notch.) Serve warm.

Daiquiri Soufflé

MAKES 1 LARGE SOUFFLÉ

The main flavors in this grand soufflé are lime and rum—it's practically a daiquiri! These flavors also pair beautifully with white chocolate. White chocolate gets a bad rap for being too sweet, but once melted, it's one of the best ways to achieve a silky texture in desserts while carrying other flavors. There are several ways to make a soufflé, but Julia Child said to make a bouillon, so that's what I do: I make a "gravy" of the milk, flour, and butter; then I add white chocolate and the fixings—the lime and the rum; last, I fold in the whipped egg white meringue. It is baked, and voilà! A stately, tall, and airy soufflé.

---

2 tablespoons (28g) **unsalted butter**, plus softened butter for the soufflé dish

3 tablespoons (30g) **granulated sugar**, plus 2 tablespoons for the soufflé dish

3½ ounces **white chocolate, finely chopped**

1 tablespoon plus 1½ teaspoons **all-purpose flour**

⅔ cup (160ml) **whole milk**

3 large **eggs**, separated, plus 1 large **egg white**

1 teaspoon (5ml) **vanilla extract**

1 teaspoon (5ml) **rum extract**

2 tablespoons (30ml) **rum** (optional)

2 tablespoons grated **zest** from 4 small limes

Pinch of **kosher salt**

¼ teaspoon **cream of tartar**

1. Preheat the oven to 375°F and place a rack in the bottom third of the oven. Prepare a 2-quart soufflé dish by smearing it with softened butter and dusting with 2 tablespoons sugar. Turn the dish upside down to tap out any excess sugar. (The soufflé will use the sugar like the rungs of a ladder to climb up the side of the dish, so don't miss any spots.)

2. Melt the white chocolate in 30-second intervals in the microwave or in a double boiler atop simmering water.

3. Add the flour to a medium saucepan over medium heat. Pour in a little milk and whisk until it forms a thick paste, then pour in the remaining milk. Add the 2 tablespoons butter and whisk until thickened like gravy and just starting to boil, whisking constantly for an additional 2 minutes. Remove the pan from the heat and continue to whisk for an additional 2 minutes so that the mixture cools slightly.

4. While whisking the gravy with one hand, stir in the yolks, one by one, whisking constantly so they don't scramble. Stir in the melted chocolate, the vanilla, rum extract, rum (if using), lime zest, and salt.

5. In the bowl of a stand mixer fitted with the whisk attachment (or in a large bowl, if using a hand mixer), whisk the egg whites and cream of tartar on low speed until foamy, about 2 minutes. Increase the speed to medium and whisk until soft peaks form (you know you have soft peaks when the egg whites appear light, fluffy, and slightly

RECIPE CONTINUES

hold their shape). Then, sprinkle in the 3 tablespoons sugar. Continue to beat on high speed until you have a glossy meringue with stiff peaks; they will form a small hook when you stick a butter knife or pastry spatula straight down into the meringue and pull it straight up. (See page 125 for more on making meringue.)

6. Use a rubber spatula to stir one-fourth of the meringue into the egg yolk mixture. Fold the remaining egg whites carefully into the egg yolk mixture, folding just until no streaks remain. You may get a little workout here—if there are lots of large lumps of glossy egg whites, just keep folding until they smooth out.

7. Pour the mixture into the prepared soufflé dish and gently smooth the top. Run your finger around the inside top lip of the soufflé dish, which will create an edge and encourage the soufflé to rise. There should be at least 1 inch of headspace at the top. Bake until the soufflé rises over the top of the dish and the edges are set, but it still jiggles in the middle when gently shaken, about 23 to 25 minutes.

8. Serve immediately because the *soufflé does not wait.*

VARIATION

Dark Chocolate Orange Soufflé
Replace the white chocolate with 4 ounces of bittersweet chocolate and increase the granulated sugar from 3 tablespoons to 6 tablespoons. Use the zest from 1 orange instead of the limes and substitute orange liqueur for the rum. Bake 23 to 25 minutes, until puffed with chocolaty aromas and just a slight wiggle in the center. Serve with a drizzle of Creamy Caramel (page 272) and Vanilla Whipped Cream (page 274) or ice cream.

The Soufflé
Does Not Wait

Some opportunities are like soufflés. They come out of the oven appearing tall, proud, and towering over the edge of a pretty ceramic dish. But if you admire it for too long, considering whether or not to indulge, that proud soufflé will have collapsed into a dense mass, resembling more of a Midwestern casserole than a star of the French pastry world.

It was July 2017 when a straight-from-the-oven metaphorical soufflé appeared in my inbox: an email from a casting agent. It was the day after my thirty-second birthday, and I was walking home from church, trying to reconcile the pastor's sermon on faith with my birthday-induced, what-am-I-doing-with-my-life funk.

In that email, the casting agent for *The Great American Baking Show* explained that she had found me on Instagram and asked if I would be interested in auditioning for the show. She said they were looking for home bakers who could make puff pastry and pie alike, and she thought I fit the bill. I had never actually heard of *The Great American Baking Show,* but I was a huge fan of its quirky British counterpart, *The Great British Bake Off.* The email said the show would be airing prime time on ABC, which was all I needed to hear to know this was the real deal. The casting agent called me that afternoon for a phone interview, asking me if I had plans that week. I did. It was Fourth of July and I was going to a friend's wedding in the Dominican Republic. I had already paid for the trip in full.

The casting agent told me she was going to pass my information on to the producers, and maybe they would invite me to continue the audition process—or maybe not. There was only one audition left in Los Angeles, and it was *that* weekend. As much as I wanted to go to the wedding, I knew this was my one shot. I had spent too many early mornings and late nights baking for my blog and Instagram account to let this opportunity slip away just because I had travel plans. So, I stood by—waiting to hear.

Over the next two days, my heart stopped a bit with each incoming call, anxiously hoping to see a number from a 323/Los Angeles area code. *Ring!* It was my mother. Yet another ring—this time, it was a telemarketer. *RING!* It was my mom (again).

The morning of July 5, before heading to work, I packed a small carry-on with bikinis, sunglasses, and mosquito repellent. My 7 P.M. flight to Santiago was confirmed, but I still hadn't heard from the producers. I sent a desperate email to the casting agent—my lone contact thus far in the process. "Hey! I'll be boarding my flight around six in the evening, so if you could please let me know if it's a 'yay' or 'nay' before I head to the airport, I would so appreciate it!"

Still no word. I left for JFK. Before my flight took off, I checked my phone one last time—still nothing. I swallowed that dream and tried to relax into the flight and prepare for a fun weekend with friends, a sufficient antidote to not moving forward with the audition process.

When our flight landed in Santiago, I checked my phone to make sure that my shuttle would be waiting for me. To my surprise, I had a *voice mail*. A producer had called me, casually inviting me to Los Angeles. I'd need to board a plane to L.A. the next day. There was one obvious snafu: I was in the Dominican Republic.

I never boarded the shuttle at the airport. Even before deplaning, I booked my ticket *back* to New York City. I had just hours to fly home, bake macarons and a loaf of bread to bring to the audition (no small feat!), and make myself "TV ready." But I did it.

Some windows of opportunity are small, but you've got to dive in and bet big. I'm still learning to recognize the soufflés in my life—to indulge and savor each bite without hesitation. Because you never know exactly when a soufflé will fall—and like all ephemeral things, it invariably will. The soufflé does not wait for anyone.

Lemon-Honey Madeleines

MAKES 2 DOZEN MADELEINES

I traveled to Dijon, France, the summer following my freshman year of college to complete the last of my mandatory foreign language courses. Dijon is the center of the Burgundy region, and the friendly Dijonnaise were more like Southerners than their cosmopolitan Parisian counterparts. We picked up local accents: *oui* became *ouaaais*. We were fueled by kirs (Dijon's signature drink of crème de cassis liqueur and white wine); smeared grainy Dijon mustard on everything; and became experts in eating madeleines—the spongy, humpbacked pastries that look like shells and resemble the yellow hat worn by my favorite children's book character of the same name.

Our resident professors Colin and Carole invited us every week to share a pastry and check in—group therapy of sorts. Madeleines were de rigueur, and as I sipped tea, we shared the highs and lows of studying abroad, as well as how the excitement of our initial arrival was met with the frustrations of living in a foreign country and homesickness. But if you stick it out and lean on your community, you can make it over that hump and reach equilibrium and enjoyment. This sage advice extends far beyond studying abroad, and I remind myself of it often.

I fell in love with France during that trip, and before heading back to L.A., I changed my major from pre-med to French. I had no desire to start my sophomore year with organic chemistry when there was Voltaire to read and more French pastries to discover.

These madeleines bring me back to Dijon. They are speckled with lemon zest—the perfect complement to the honey-sweetened, spongy tea cakes. The batter needs to rest overnight, so they're perfect to make ahead. To ensure you get the characteristic "hump," be sure to chill the pan and transfer to a sufficiently hot oven.

4 large **eggs**

¾ cup (150g) **granulated sugar**

2 tablespoons (40g) **honey**

2 tablespoons grated **lemon zest** (from about 2 lemons)

1⅓ cups (160g) **cake flour**, plus more for dusting the pans

2 teaspoons **baking powder**

½ teaspoon **kosher salt**

¾ cup (1½ sticks/170g) **unsalted butter**, melted, plus softened butter for the pans

1. In the bowl of a stand mixer fitted with the whisk attachment (or in a large bowl, if using a hand mixer), beat the eggs, sugar, honey, and lemon zest on high speed until pale and frothy, about 3 minutes. Remove the bowl from the stand mixer and sift in the cake flour, baking powder, and salt. Use a rubber spatula to fold in the dry ingredients until just combined and no streaks of flour remain. Add the melted butter and stir with a rubber spatula until just combined. Cover the bowl with plastic and let rest in the refrigerator overnight.

2. Preheat the oven to 400°F and place a rack in the middle of the oven. Prepare the madeleine pan by smearing the depressions with softened butter and then dusting with a little cake flour. Place the pan in the freezer for 10 minutes so the butter will harden.

3. Remove the batter from the refrigerator and spoon it into the mold three-fourths full (don't spread the batter—the heat from the oven will do that). Transfer the pan to the

storage These are excellent straight out of the oven, or allow to cool completely before storing in an airtight container at room temperature for up to 4 days.

oven and bake just until puffed in the center and golden along the edges, 8 to 10 minutes. Repeat with the remaining pan.

4. Cool the madeleines in the pans on a cooling rack for 5 minutes. Invert the pans and let cool slightly more on a rack. Serve warm or cool.

A Very Dramatic Crêpe Cake

MAKES 1 LAYER CAKE

Thin crêpes are stacked and sandwiched with cream in this crêpes-meet-layered-cake mashup. The double batch of crêpes makes it visually stunning. While the assembled cake rests in the refrigerator, the cream melds with the layers, producing a lighter version of both crêpes and cake. You can top this with whipped cream and raspberries, but it's also delicious as is.

2 batches (about 4 cups total) **"Cheat" Pastry Cream** (page 277)

2½ cup (600ml) **heavy cream**

36 (2 batches) **Crêpes** (page 76)

make ahead The cake can be assembled up to 2 days in advance. The crêpes may be prepared in advance as well, then cooled and stacked.

1. Place 2 cups of the heavy cream in the bowl of a stand mixer or large bowl (if using a hand mixer). Whip on medium until soft peaks form, about 6 minutes. Fold the whipped cream into the cheat pastry cream until combined and smooth.

2. Place a single crêpe on a cake plate or cake board. Measure a scant ⅓ cup of the filling onto the crêpe and use a small, offset spatula or a butter knife to smooth it into an even layer. Place the next crêpe on top and continue layering until you are out of filling (you will have several crêpes left over, which are perfect for snacking while the cake chills).

3. Wrap the cake in plastic and refrigerate for at least 6 hours so the filling can set.

4. When ready to serve, whip the remaining ½ cup heavy cream in the bowl of the stand mixer fitted with the whisk attachment until medium-stiff peaks form. Dollop the whipped cream on top of the cake. Slice and serve like a traditional layered cake.

note Use 4 wooden skewers to secure the cake so that the tall layers won't slide off the cake.

Cake Pan Quiche Lorraine

MAKES ONE 8- OR 9-INCH QUICHE

"I thought you did really great work, and *I* believe that you contributed a great deal to our law firm this summer." It was the emphasis on "I" that gave me pause. A warning sign that bad news was coming. He continued, "But we [the partners] talked it over, and we aren't going to be able to give you an offer."

This was the brief "no offer" phone call I received as I wrapped up my summer internship at a law firm. It was the summer of 2009 and in the midst of a full-on recession. Law firms were laying off attorneys who were already there—not hiring summer associates was the least of their worries.

I was a just-turned-twenty-four-year-old and I was crushed. This was going to be the grand finale of my many years of schooling: a job at a prestigious law firm, making enough money that I could pay back my student loans and eat at nice restaurants without worrying about how much the entrée costs. I decided to take my destiny into my own hands and find the silver lining. And that's how I ended up in Paris with two roommates—Victor and Émilie. Each evening, the three of us would make dinner together. And then we would sit down and *eat* together. This wasn't extraordinary among roommates in France— cooking dinner together was the norm.

We cooked every night, and I learned a new effortless, breezy approach to weeknight dinners. A quiche was as simple as unrolling a round of pie crust and fitting it into a pan with some whisked eggs, cream, cheese, and crisped lardons.

A tart pan is too shallow to hold in all the delicious possible fillings of a quiche, so I do something sacrilegious: I make it in a cake pan! For an easy weeknight dinner, I use a ready-made store-bought crust, but a homemade Flaky Pie Crust (page 140) would elevate this from weeknight to Wow! Add a simple salad for a complete meal (energetic, optimistic French roommates not included).

4 ounces (120g) diced **pancetta** or **bacon**

2 **shallots** or 1 large **onion**, finely chopped

3 large **eggs**

1 cup (240ml) **heavy cream**

½ cup (120ml) **whole milk**

½ teaspoon **kosher salt**

¼ teaspoon **ground black pepper**

¼ teaspoon **grated nutmeg**

⅛ teaspoon **cayenne pepper**

1 cup (235g) grated **Gruyère, Swiss,** or **cheddar cheese**

1 store-bought round of **pie crust**, or 1 disk of dough for **Flaky Pie Crust** (page 140), in a 9-inch cake pan or springform pan and partially baked (see page 173)

---

1. Preheat the oven to 375°F and place a rack in the center of the oven.

2. Add the pancetta to a skillet set over medium heat and sauté, stirring often, until it's crispy and the fat has melted and is pooling around the pancetta bits, about 5 minutes. Transfer the crispy pancetta to a paper towel–lined plate.

3. Pour out any oil in excess of a tablespoon from the skillet. Add the shallots and sauté over medium heat, stirring occasionally, until they are translucent, about 7 minutes.

4. In a medium bowl, whisk the eggs, cream, milk, salt, black pepper, nutmeg, and cayenne until combined.

5. Sprinkle the pancetta, shallots, and cheese in an even layer over the crust. Pour the egg-cream mixture through a sieve into the crust (this ensures your filling is silky smooth).

6. Bake the quiche until the filling is just set (give it a little shake and the center will barely jiggle) and golden on top, 35 to 40 minutes. Remove from the oven and let cool for 10 minutes before slicing and serving.

storage Leftovers can be stored in the refrigerator, covered, for up to 3 days.

Vanilla Ganache Macarons

MAKES 1 DOZEN MACARONS

Macarons have a reputation for being tricky to make; however, with the right equipment (a digital scale, stand mixer, piping bag, and a 10- or 12-point round piping tip), you'll find they're more achievable than they look. Making macarons is more technical than making brownies, but you master some great foundational concepts along the way, like folding the meringue into the batter and piping skills. There's a world of fillings and flavors for macarons. I prefer the ganache-based fillings: a simple emulsion of cream and chocolate, which is the smooth and creamy perfect balance with the almondy macaron shell. But I also love tangy curd-filled and simple jam-filled macarons. These macarons need an hour to dry out before baking, and the filling needs about 2 hours to thicken.

FOR THE FILLING

⅓ cup (80ml) **heavy cream**

1 **vanilla bean**

8 ounces good-quality **white chocolate**, finely chopped

1 tablespoon **unsalted butter**, room temperature

FOR THE SHELLS

1 cup (96g) finely ground **almond flour**

1⅔ cups (200g) **confectioners' sugar**

3 large **egg whites** (90g), room temperature (see page 190)

½ teaspoon **kosher salt**

⅓ cup (65g) **granulated sugar**

Gel food coloring of your choice (optional)

1. Make the vanilla ganache filling: Add the heavy cream to a small saucepan. Cut the vanilla bean in half lengthwise and use the tip of a knife to open the pod. Scrape the seeds into the cream and stir, then add the vanilla bean pod. Heat the heavy cream until just simmering. Immediately remove from the heat and cover to allow the vanilla to infuse the cream for 15 minutes. Heat the chocolate in the microwave in 30-second intervals, stirring between each, until melted. Remove the vanilla bean pod from the cream, squeezing it to ensure you get all of the vanilla flavor and cream from the pod. Rinse the pod and reserve for another use. Add the cream to the melted white chocolate and stir in small circles until smooth and emulsified. Add the tablespoon of softened butter and stir until smooth. Set aside, covered, at room temperature, while preparing the shells.

2. Make the shells: Sift the almond flour and confectioners' sugar through a fine mesh sieve into a large bowl and set aside.

3. Place the egg whites and salt in the bowl of a stand mixer fitted with the whisk attachment. Start whisking on medium speed until frothy and soft peaks form, about 2 minutes.

4. Add the granulated sugar slowly and increase the speed to high. Beat until stiff peaks form, 2 to 4 minutes. To find stiff peaks, stick a butter knife into the meringue mixture and pull upward; the meringue should be able to hold its shape. Add the gel food coloring, if using, and beat until just evenly dispersed in the meringue.

RECIPE CONTINUES

5. Add the whipped egg whites to the almond flour mixture. Begin to fold the meringue into the almond flour mixture until incorporated. Continue stirring the meringue until it starts to shine and slowly falls off the spatula without breaking when lifted but also holds its shape, similar to lava. This might take a few minutes of folding—don't rush it. Achieving the right consistency is paramount to getting shiny, smooth macaron shells.

6. Line a baking sheet with a silicone baking mat or parchment paper. Transfer half of the mixture to a piping bag fitted with a 10- or 12-point tip. Pipe the batter onto the prepared baking sheet, making the macarons about 1½ inches in circumference, and spacing them 2 inches apart from one another. Once a full sheet of macarons have been piped, pick up the baking sheet and drop it on a table from about 5 inches high; repeat two or three times. This is important to knock any air bubbles out. Let the shells sit undisturbed for 30 minutes to 1 hour to dry out. You should be able to lightly touch them without the macaron paste sticking to your fingers (a thin skin will develop on top). Repeat with the remaining mixture.

7. Preheat the oven to 300°F. Bake the shells for 14 to 17 minutes, until they are dry to the touch. Remove the pan from the oven. Transfer the pan to a cooling rack to cool completely. Carefully remove the macaron shells from the pan by gently peeling the parchment or silicone baking mat back. (If you don't remove them quickly, they may end up sticking.) Pair similar-sized macaron shells together before filling.

8. Assemble the macarons: Pipe the filling in the center of half of the macaron shells. Place a shell on top of each, flat-side down. Enjoy immediately, or place the assembled macarons in an airtight container and refrigerate overnight or up to 5 days. Remove the macarons from the refrigerator about 10 minutes before serving. The macarons should be served at room temperature.

---

notes Macarons require precision, so for best results, I recommend using a scale to measure ingredients. Using a stand mixer is also best for whipping up the egg whites for the meringue because it allows you to have both hands free and is more powerful than a hand mixer.

---

storage Place the assembled macarons in an airtight container and refrigerate overnight or up to 5 days. Remove from the refrigerator about 10 minutes before serving.

See page 27 for video tutorial instructions on piping macarons (and using a piping bag!).

Practice Bakes Perfect

Years before I auditioned for *The Great American Baking Show*, I decided to start a macaron business. In fact, I decided to sell macarons before I knew how to make them. I was convinced that with enough practice, I could master the tricky little pastries. With Pierre Hermés's *Macarons* book as my guide (it was in French), I made batch after batch of macarons, and batch after batch went into the garbage. I knew this couldn't be a faulty recipe—the whole book was devoted to macarons!—so I continued the "bake and toss" before realizing my oven was not calibrated correctly. The temperature was much higher than the setting indicated, causing my macaron shells to burn and crack.

A lesson I learned from thirteen years of piano lessons proved true: practice ~~makes~~ *bakes* perfect. I soon mastered making macarons, along with making Italian meringue (a daunting process of pouring boiling hot sugar into whipping egg whites), using a pastry bag, and even emulsifying ganache. Macarons were the canvas on which I painted all my pastry whims, from traditional flavors like vanilla to more eclectic ones like sweet potato pie.

I was looking into renting commercial kitchen space when I came across Hot Bread Kitchen in New York City, which was a program that incubates young food-preneurs. Submitting a business plan was part of the application, so I checked out a book from the library, *How to Write a Business Plan*, and then I wrote one!

Before I knew it, I was selling macarons at the Dekalb market, and eventually the historic New Amsterdam Market. I was selling out and making a name for myself. People liked them—no, *loved* them. I had loyal customers and was covered in local newspapers. I kept it up for a few months. Hustling at markets. Walking around the city, going into bakeries to see if they'd be willing to buy wholesale. Eventually, it got to the point where I was taking *too* many days off of work from my day job as a lawyer (I'd take 2 to 3 days off to prepare for a weekend at the market). I was selling out, but the ingredients were so expensive. There wasn't a feasible way to make it work with my lack of storage and my schlepping oversized baking pans from our Murray Hill apartment all the way to East Harlem (and back again, except with 1500 delicate macarons in tow).

I was straddling two worlds: being a lawyer and being a macaron hustler. I had spent too much time in school and had taken two too many bar exams to give that up completely—plus I didn't think I had the business savvy to make it work. So I hung up my apron and, for the next five years, I focused on building my career as an attorney. But little did I know that my future in the food business was just beginning.

Buckwheat Galettes

MAKES 10 GALETTES

Every college student has a late-night spot for food—the one place that's guaranteed to be open when the party is over. While I was living in L.A., that place was Roscoe's, where I'd indulge in the Carole C. Special—one succulent chicken breast and a golden waffle. In Paris, that late-night place was the Latin Quarter, and the food was galettes: savory buckwheat crêpes stuffed with Emmentaler cheese, ham, and potato slices, and topped with a fried egg. This hearty street food was the perfect antidote to a night out at the discotheques of Paris.

Now I enjoy galettes any time of day. These galettes (not to be confused with the free-form pies of the same name) have a short, tender bite, since the buckwheat flour doesn't have gluten. They are cooked until crispy—the lacy browned and crunchy edges indicate a well-made one. Though they might be filled with savory ingredients and fit the bill as late-night street food, their appeal doesn't end there. I have come to love them just as much with a little cheese, folded into a rectangle, and served with a simply dressed salad for lunch.

1¼ cups (150g) **buckwheat flour**

¾ cup (90g) **all-purpose flour**

1½ teaspoons **kosher salt**

1 large **egg**

1¼ cups (300ml) **whole milk**

1¼ cups (300ml) **water**

5 tablespoons (70g) **unsalted butter**

1. Combine the flours, salt, egg, milk, and water in a blender. Blend on low speed for 10 seconds, then raise the speed to medium and blend for 10 seconds longer. Stop the blender and use a spatula to scrape the bottom and sides—the buckwheat flour likes to clump—then blend on medium speed for another 10 seconds.

2. A well-seasoned cast-iron skillet will give you the best nonstick surface—it's the closest replica of the steel crêpe pans used by home cooks in France. Heat over fairly high heat (or one or two notches from total high). When hot and smoking (this could take a few minutes), add ½ tablespoon of the butter. The butter should sizzle and bubble as it hits the pan. Tilt the pan and rotate it to get the butter to coat the surface evenly as it melts. Work quickly—within a few seconds, the butter will start to brown.

3. Place ⅓ cup of the batter in the hot skillet. (I like to pour with my left hand, so that my right hand—my dominant hand—is ready to immediately swirl the batter around the pan.) Be sure to use a glove or kitchen towel— cast-iron skillet handles are hot! The batter will start to set immediately, so swirl the best you can—but, it's okay if you don't get a perfect circle. Maybe you'll have an oval, or maybe your galette will have tentacles—that's fine! Set a timer for 2 minutes. The edges will start to brown, and tiny holes will form on the surface, first at the edges and then all over. (The lacy edges with crispy textured bits may be the tastiest part of a galette.) After

RECIPE CONTINUES

2 minutes, carefully run a large, offset spatula under the bottom of the galette and flip it. If the galettes start to cook too quickly, reduce the heat to medium for the remaining galettes.

4. If you're serving the galette au naturel, cook the second side until set, 30 seconds to 1 minute. Carefully transfer to a plate and continue making the galettes, stacking one on top of the previous, until you use up the batter, adding more butter to the pan between crepes as needed. Serve.

HEC Galette Complète (The Parisian "BEC")
New York City is famous for the "BEC," a bacon, egg, and cheese sandwich. It's a grab-and-go favorite from the bodegas. Paris's version is the HEC—ham, egg, and cheese, but instead of being served on a griddled Kaiser roll, the stuffing is folded into a buckwheat galette. In Paris's Latin Quarter, they even add some sliced potato for an extra-hearty treat.

To make the Parisian version, follow the instructions for making the galettes through the end of step 3. After you flip the galette, add the toppings: ¼ cup grated Emmentaler cheese, a slice of ham, and a few slices of cooked potato. Let cook another 30 seconds, then fold the four edges over to make a square and nestle a fried egg in the center of the square. Cook to set the egg, then transfer to a plate to serve.

Canelés

MAKES 1 DOZEN CANELÉS

For this recipe, the batter must be made 24 to 48 hours before baking. Also, you will need canelé molds. Nothing will yeild results like copper molds, but they are pricey! Silicone is an acceptable alternative.

---

1 **vanilla bean**

2 cups (480ml) **whole milk**

3½ tablespoons (50g) **unsalted butter**

2 cups (250g) **confectioners' sugar**

¾ cup plus 1 tablespoon (100g) **all-purpose flour**

2 large **eggs** plus 2 large **egg yolks**

3 tablespoons (45ml) **orange liqueur** or **rum**

Grated zest from ½ **orange**

---

1. Cut the vanilla bean in half lengthwise and use a spoon to scrape out the seeds. Add the seeds, the scraped pod, 1½ cups of the milk, and the butter to a medium saucepan over medium-high heat. Bring to a boil, then remove from the heat, cover the pot, and allow the vanilla pod to infuse the mixture for 10 minutes.

2. Meanwhile, sift the confectioners' sugar into a large bowl, then whisk in the flour. Add the remaining ½ cup milk and whisk until combined.

3. Use your fingers to remove the vanilla pod, squeezing to release any warm milk (save the pod—you'll use it in the next step). Pour the warm milk into the flour mixture and whisk to combine.

4. Add the eggs, egg yolks, orange liqueur, and orange zest and whisk until the mixture is smooth and well combined. Add the empty vanilla pod, cover the bowl with plastic, and refrigerate for at least 24 hours and up to 48 hours.

5. Preheat the oven to 425°F. Remove the batter from the refrigerator and give it a gentle stir in case it has separated. Pour the batter into the cups of the canelé mold, leaving a headspace of about ⅜ inch at the top of each mold cup. Bake for 30 minutes, then reduce the heat to 375°F and bake until the tops are so dark and caramelized that they appear burnt, an additional 25 minutes. Remove from the oven and immediately unmold the canelés onto a wire rack to cool before serving.

---

storage Canelés are best the day they are made, but they can be refrigerated for up to 5 days and frozen for up to 2 months. When you're ready to serve, refresh them in a 450°F oven, uncovered, for 5 minutes or until hot.

How to prepare copper Canelé moulds

Brush a thin coating of melted shortening into each mould. Invert the mould to allow excess shortening to drip out. Freeze the moulds for 15 minutes prior to use.

Hitchiking
in Bordeaux

It was 25 degrees Fahrenheit, and I was stranded on the side of the road deep in the backwoods of Bordeaux. I glanced at the bus schedule; no bus was coming. In fact, no cars were even coming. The January winds pierced my face. I was a long way from sunny California where I spent the previous seven years in college and law school. I was on a recession-imposed gap year of sorts.

Before this stint in France, I was living in L.A. with my sister, who unexpectedly lost her fiancé the year prior. My boyfriend of four years matched in a residency program on what felt like the other side of the world: New York City. I was afraid my sister would feel abandoned if I left, and that my boyfriend would feel like he wasn't a priority if I stayed. I didn't want to let either of them down, so instead, I let both of them down. I didn't stay in L.A., and I didn't move to New York—at least not yet. I returned to the place that had brought me joy through discovery and unexpected community—France.

I was living on the outskirts of Paris, working part time as a language assistant. I decided to go to Bordeaux for the weekend, January temperatures be damned. Bordeaux is no Napa. There are no busloads of tourists, and elaborate tasting rooms are rare. Most wineries are by appointment only—a chance to have an intimate glimpse of the winemaking process. To me, winemakers were more akin to farmers than sommeliers—learning from them is for the food obsessed who geek out over *terroir*. These were my people. I learned that back in the day, nuns used egg whites to filter wine. And the many excess egg yolks were made into the pastry darling of Bordeaux—the wine-cork-shaped canelé. With their custardy interior and their caramelized, crisp exteriors, these pastries are the perfect afternoon treat with a cup of coffee.

A rush of cold air jolted me back from daydreaming about the canelé I had enjoyed earlier that morning. I could no longer feel my fingertips or toes. After standing outside for half an hour with no plan on how to return to my hostel in Bordeaux city, a truck appeared. Without giving it much thought, I jumped up, walked closer to the edge of the road, and stuck my arm out, tilting my thumb sideways—just like they do in the movies. I was unsure if this bit of nonverbal communication would transcend the English-French language barrier.

It worked. He stopped, and I climbed into the passenger's seat with no thoughts of "stranger danger" or a potential kidnapping—just gratitude that I was out of the cold.

It's easier to travel and take risks when you're young: when you can't pay the inflated price for renting a car internationally; when you are naive enough to check the bus schedule to make sure you will make it to your vineyard appointment—even though the thought of the return ride never crosses your mind; when you have more faith than fear.

The truck driver dropped me off in Bordeaux city. I treated myself to the warmth of a bistro with a glass of sauternes and a canelé as my reward for an incredible day discussing wine and life—and for making it back into town.

COOKIES & BARS

The recipe for cookie greatness extends beyond flour, butter, and sugar—patience and consistency are also key ingredients. As a free spirit, I'm not surprised cookies weren't always my forte. I've since dealt head-on with my cookie issues, because cookies are simply too scrumptious (and portable!) to ignore.

Making cookies has taught me patience: creaming the butter and sugar takes a bit of time, and if you move too quickly, your cookies will be dense. Cookies have taught me consistency: if the cookies are the same size and are evenly spaced on the baking sheet, they will bake uniformly. While for the most part I'm still not a rules follower, when it comes to cookie making, I can be. In this chapter, you'll learn the most important cookie-making techniques.

Cookie
Hall of Fame

My first foray into the cookie business involved selling them, not baking them. I'm not sure what my motivation was for selling Girl Scout cookies other than a burgeoning desire for boundless achievement, but I took my cookie sales *very* seriously. This was the analog Girl Scout cookie world of paper order forms and door-to-door knocking. There were rules. Cookie sales started at 9 A.M. on a designated Saturday, and at 9 A.M., I would be on the first doorstep, green order form in hand, saying, "Good morning! Would you like to buy some Girl Scout cookies!?"

If I sensed any reservation, I had responses prepared. "They freeze well!" "They make excellent gifts!" My sales extended far beyond the streets of my suburban neighborhood in south Baton Rouge. The first thing I did was recruit a sales team: my mom and dad. This was no easy task because I had competition—my older sister Lucy was also selling Girl Scout cookies. My most loyal customers were the members of Greene Chapel A.M.E. Church (my home church). I'm sure they were more interested in supporting me than consuming boxes of cookies! Needless to say, I spent the next two weeks in full-blown cookie mode before turning in my order forms with all the pride a ten-year-old future Girl Scout Cookie Hall of Famer could muster.

Weeks later, after receiving the cookies, I realized that distributing hundreds and hundreds of boxes was far more challenging than filling up an order form. If only I had approached my cookie distribution with the same gumption as my cookie sales. I found myself sitting on the carpeted floor of my bedroom, surrounded by towering cases filled with boxes of Trefoils, Peanut Butter Patties, and Samoas—with no apparent owners of those cookies in sight. It was too much temptation for this sweet-toothed Girl Scout. I ended up devouring cookies from multiple boxes. With quite the tummy ache and fingers sticky from chocolate, I learned an important lesson in self-control. I also made the first critical error one can make in the food business. It's the error we've been warned about in mob movies and rap songs alike: "Don't get high on your own supply."

Red Velvet Thumbprints

MAKES 2 DOZEN COOKIES

I didn't feel connected to the baking community until I joined Instagram. The second picture I posted was of these thumbprint cookies. To my surprise, they were reposted by one of my favorite baking magazines, *Southern Living*! I got about ten followers from the repost, but it was the early affirmation that I needed to let me know my work resonated with people.

The bright red color with a hint of chocolate in these cookies fits the classic red velvet cake profile (and makes them extra festive!). Instead of the typical chocolate Kiss in the center, these thumbprints call for a cream cheese frosting. By piping the creamy white frosting into the indentations, you get the classic cone center and a creamy complement to the chewy red velvet cookie.

1¼ cups (150g) **all-purpose flour**

½ teaspoon **kosher salt**

3 tablespoons (15g) **unsweetened cocoa powder**

½ cup (1 stick/113g) **unsalted butter**, room temperature

¾ cup (150g) **granulated sugar**

1 large **egg**

1 teaspoon **red food coloring** (optional)

1 teaspoon **vanilla extract**

¼ recipe **cream cheese frosting** (see page 187)

storage Store the cookies in an airtight container for up to 3 days.

1. Preheat the oven to 325°F and place a rack in the middle of the oven. Line a baking sheet with parchment paper or a silicone baking mat.

2. Whisk together the flour and salt in a medium bowl. Sift in the cocoa powder and whisk to combine.

3. In the bowl of a stand mixer fitted with the paddle attachment, combine the butter and sugar and beat on medium speed until light and fluffy, about 2 minutes. Add the egg, food coloring (if using), and vanilla, and continue to beat until combined, an additional 1 minute, using a rubber spatula to scrape the bottom and the sides of the bowl as needed.

4. Reduce the speed to low and add the flour mixture. Mix on low speed until just combined. Scrape the bottom and sides of the bowl.

5. Scoop out 1 heaping tablespoon of the dough and roll it between your palms to form a 1-inch ball (the dough can be a little sticky!). Place the ball on the prepared baking sheet, and make more balls, keeping them 2 inches apart on the baking sheet. Use the knuckle of your index finger or the end of a wooden spoon to press an indentation in the center of each ball (don't press too deep—you don't want to poke through to the other side of the dough).

6. Bake the cookies until they appear dried out and their aroma wafts through your kitchen, about 12 minutes. Allow the cookies to cool on a rack for 5 minutes, then gently press into the center of each cookie again with your knuckle.

7. Allow to cool completely before piping or spooning the cream cheese frosting into the indentations and serving.

Tips on How
the Cookie Crumbles

I grew up in a world of foot-long, sausage-like tubes of slice-and-bake cookie dough. I was accustomed to these break-and-bake cookies, so I was always impatient when making cookies from scratch. I'd put the sugar and butter in the bowl of a stand mixer and immediately crank up the speed to high, thwacking the life (and air) out of the butter and sugar. I'd add the eggs and beat the life out of them, too. Then, I'd spoon the dough onto a baking sheet and immediately put the cookies in the oven, without chilling the dough first! And I had the nerve to wonder why my cookies were dense or would spread out so much when they hit the hot oven that they looked like puddles on the baking sheet.

If I had just left the mixer speed at medium for about 5 minutes when creaming the butter and sugar, I would have achieved that "pale and fluffy" perfection, making my cookies lighter. And if I had let the dough rest in the fridge before baking, the butter would have firmed up and the cookies would have puffed up, rather than going *melty-cookie-splat* in the oven.

Here are some other tips I learned that will help you make better cookies:

Roll 'em Thin (without stressing!)

Cookies rolled out on the kitchen counter can be hard to handle. However, if you roll out the dough between 2 sheets of wax paper and then transfer the wax paper–sandwiched dough to a baking sheet in the fridge, the butter will firm up as the dough chills and you'll be able to cut them out and transfer them to the baking sheet with ease. (I like to use an offset spatula.) If at any point the dough becomes too soft, you can stick it back in the fridge or freezer until the butter solidifies again.

Finish by Hand

A lot of my recipes say to stop the mixer before all the flour is incorporated into the dough. Stand mixers are powerful machines, and a cookie dough can quickly go from "mixed and ready" to overmixed in a heartbeat, which results in a tough cookie. The easiest fix is to finish the dough old school—take the bowl off the mixer stand and use a rubber spatula (and a little elbow grease) to finish bringing the dough together by hand.

Bake Two Sheets at Once

Most of my cookie recipes call for baking the cookies on a sheet in the middle of the oven. That often means double the baking time when you're making enough cookies to use two baking sheets. But if you want to cut that baking time in half, you can bake the two sheets at the same time by positioning them in the top and bottom thirds of the oven, and switching the trays halfway through the baking time.

Age the Dough

Like fine wines and women (!), cookie dough gets better with age. As little as 30 minutes of chilling will net positive results because it will give the butter a chance to firm up, meaning it will stay solid longer when it's in the oven and will spread less (no one wants a cookie puddle!). Also, refrigerating the dough gives the flour time to soak up the liquid so the dough is evenly moistened, resulting in better browning and a tastier cookie. While 30 minutes is the minimum, you can age your cookie dough up to three days in the fridge—the dough will just get better and better. Be sure the dough is well wrapped in plastic so it doesn't dry out.

Use Suga, Suga!

A lot of cookie recipes call for both granulated (white) sugar and brown sugar. Both sugar types play important roles: the granulated sugar adds structure, and the molasses from the brown sugar adds complex flavor and moisture, ensuring your cookie retains a tender, soft bite.

Chocolate Shortbread Cookies

MAKES 2 DOZEN COOKIES

These delicate cookies are simple, chocolaty, and buttery. They're the perfect base for a sandwich cookie, but are also delectable on their own. You can add ½ teaspoon of mint extract for a chocolate-peppermint shortbread.

2⅔ cups (333g) **all-purpose flour**

⅓ cup (25g) **unsweetened natural cocoa powder** (not Dutch-processed)

½ teaspoon **kosher salt**

¼ teaspoon **baking powder**

1 cup (2 sticks/226g) **unsalted butter**, room temperature

⅔ cup (133g) **granulated sugar**

1 large **egg**, room temperature

1 teaspoon **vanilla extract**

1. Add the flour to a large bowl. Sift in the cocoa powder. Add the salt and baking powder and use a whisk or fork to combine.

2. In the bowl of a stand mixer fitted with the paddle attachment, combine the butter and sugar. Beat on medium speed to cream the butter and sugar until the mixture becomes fluffy and very pale, about 3 minutes. Turn the mixer off and scrape down the side and bottom of the bowl.

3. Add the egg and vanilla and keep beating until it's thoroughly combined, about 1 more minute. If the mixture starts to look separated, beat an extra minute or so until it comes together and is the consistency of a thick cake batter.

4. Reduce the mixer speed to low and add the dry mixture a large spoonful at a time. It will appear crumbly at first, like pie dough that hasn't yet come together. Keep mixing until the dough starts to come together in large dough-like clumps. You are looking for the Goldilocks principle of mixing here: not too much, not too little—but just enough. Be careful not to overmix. If there is still flour at the bottom of the bowl that has yet to be incorporated, you can finish it by hand and use a large, sturdy spatula to fold the flour into this stiff dough.

5. Tip the dough out onto a work surface, press into a ball, and divide into 2 equal halves.

6. Roll one mass of dough between two 14-inch-long pieces of parchment or wax paper to a ¼-inch thickness. Slide the paper-sandwiched dough onto a baking sheet and refrigerate until the dough is firm, about 30 minutes. Repeat with the second mass of dough.

7. Remove the first sheet of dough from the refrigerator. Line the baking sheet with parchment paper. Stamp out cookies using a 2¾-inch round cookie cutter, and place the cookies on the baking sheet. If the dough sticks to the cutter, coat it in flour and continue cutting. Reroll the scraps by sandwiching them between sheets of parchment, then cut out the shapes and continue until all the dough is used. Repeat for the second sheet of chilled dough.

8. Return the baking sheets with the cutout dough rounds to the refrigerator to chill, at least 15 minutes.

9. Preheat the oven to 350°F and place a rack in the middle of the oven (or in the top and bottom thirds, if baking both sheets at the same time).

10. Transfer the baking sheet(s) to the oven and bake until the aroma of chocolate wafts through your kitchen and the cookies appear dry around the edges, 10 to 12 minutes (it can be tricky to tell when chocolate dough is baked since you can't go by color; see page 160).

11. Remove from the oven and transfer the baking sheet(s) to a cooling rack. (If baking the sheets separately, repeat for the second sheet of cutout cookies.) Let the cookies cool on the baking sheet for 10 minutes—if you try to remove them too soon, the delicate and thin cookies will break from the pressure of your fingertips.

12. Gently slide the parchment paper with the cookies onto a cooling rack and let cool completely before serving.

---

storage These can be stored in an airtight container at room temperature for up to 1 week.

Rolling Pin Rings!

This simple tool will ensure your cookie dough and pie dough is rolled exactly ⅛ inch, ¼ inch, or even ½ inch! Rolling pin rings fit onto both ends of your pin, keeping dough even and taking the guesswork out of rolling dough to a desired thickness.

German Chocolate Sandwich Cookies

MAKES 1 DOZEN SANDWICH COOKIES

With these chocolate shortbread cookies sandwiching a traditional German chocolate cake filling (made with shredded coconut, pecans, and a stovetop creamy caramel), they have all the festive deliciousness of their namesake cake. They were inspired by the ones I made during a crazy two-hour cookie challenge on *The Great American Baking Show.* I was always looking for ways to add pizzazz to my desserts—this was television, after all. So, I decided to buy a fully mature coconut to grate over the chocolate-striped cookies. I used a mallet to crack open the coconut at our hotel and brought the pieces to the set, then emphatically sprinkled the fresh coconut meat like snowflakes falling onto the cookies. But you don't need to go through all that trouble! Instead, drizzle them with chocolate, chopped pecans, and toasted coconut to lend an equally elegant look.

¾ cup (85g) finely chopped **pecans** (see Note on page 114)

1 cup (85g) **sweetened** or **unsweetened shredded coconut**

2 large **egg yolks**

¾ cup (180ml) **evaporated milk**

½ teaspoon **vanilla extract**

¾ cup (150g) **granulated sugar**

6 tablespoons (85g) **unsalted butter**

24 **Chocolate Shortbread Cookies** (page 110)

2 ounces **sweetened chocolate of choice** (milk, white, or dark)

1. Preheat the oven to 350°F and place a rack in the middle of the oven. Line a baking sheet with parchment paper. Spread the pecans in an even layer. Bake until they are fragrant and just starting to brown, 5 to 7 minutes (keep a close eye on them—they can burn easily). Transfer to a plate to cool.

2. Spread the coconut in an even, thin layer on the parchment-lined baking sheet. Bake until starting to brown, about 5 minutes.

3. Add the egg yolks, evaporated milk, vanilla, and sugar to a medium saucepan and whisk to combine.

4. Cut the butter into large, even pieces so it will melt evenly. Add them to the saucepan and set the saucepan over medium heat.

5. Use a heatproof rubber spatula or wooden spoon to stir occasionally until the butter melts. The mixture will start to bubble around the edges—use the spatula to scrape the bottom of the pan continually to prevent burning. The mixture will become bubbly across the surface and turn a deep marigold color (if bubbling too vigorously, turn the heat down to medium-low). When the butter mixture darkens to deep tan and thickens, remove the pan from the heat, about 12 minutes in total.

6. Set aside a small handful of the toasted pecans and toasted coconut for garnish. Stir the remainder of the pecans and coconut into the butter mixture in the saucepan. Transfer to a medium bowl and let sit until cool enough to handle, about 15 minutes.

RECIPE CONTINUES

7. Place half the cookies on your work surface. Spread 1½ teaspoons of the pecan-coconut filling onto each cookie. Set another cookie on top and gently press to sandwich the filling.

8. Melt the chocolate in a heatproof bowl in the microwave, stirring in 15-second intervals until melted. Place the sandwiched cookies on a cooling rack with parchment or wax paper underneath (this will make cleanup easier!). Drizzle the cookies with the melted chocolate and sprinkle with the reserved pecans and coconut before serving.

storage Store the cookies in an airtight container at room temperature for up to 1 week.

---

note Finely chopping the pecans is important because they go into the filling for the cookies. If you have large pieces of nuts, that makes spreading the filling more difficult. The filling makes enough for a double batch.

Gingerbread Cookies

MAKES 16 COOKIES

These cake-like cookies have all the delicious gingerbread flavor and none of the drama that comes with gingerbread house collapses! They are adapted from the gingerbread dough I made on *The Great American Baking Show*. The only difference is that these are drop cookies, so there's more leavening (egg and a little baking soda). I also added some crystallized ginger, which gives a flavorful punch to this cookie, as does the black pepper.

1¾ cups (210g) **all-purpose flour**

2 teaspoons **baking soda**

2 teaspoons **ground ginger**

1 teaspoon **ground cinnamon**

¼ teaspoon **ground cloves**

¼ teaspoon **ground allspice**

½ teaspoon **kosher salt**

⅛ teaspoon **black pepper**

6 tablespoons (85g) **unsalted butter**, room temperature

¼ cup (50g) firmly packed **light** or **dark brown sugar**

¼ cup (85g) **molasses**

1 tablespoon (5g) grated or finely chopped **fresh ginger**

1 large **egg**

¼ cup (40g) **crystallized ginger**, chopped into ¼- to ⅛-inch pieces

¼ cup (50g) **demerara sugar**

---

make ahead The dough can be refrigerated, wrapped tightly in plastic, for up to 3 days before baking.

1. Preheat the oven to 350°F and place a rack in the middle of the oven. Line 2 baking sheets with parchment paper.

2. In a medium or large bowl, whisk together the flour, baking soda, ginger, cinnamon, cloves, allspice, salt, and pepper.

3. To the bowl of a stand mixer fitted with the paddle attachment, or a large bowl and using a wooden spoon, add the softened butter, brown sugar, molasses, and fresh ginger. Cream the butter and sweeteners on medium speed for about 2 minutes. Add the egg and continue to cream until combined, an additional 1 to 2 minutes. (If the mixture appears broken, don't worry—it will come together once the flour is added.)

4. With the mixer running on low speed, add the flour mixture a heaping spoonful at a time until the last bit of flour has been added, then turn the mixer off. (It's okay if all the flour hasn't been fully incorporated.) Remove the bowl from the stand and use a sturdy rubber spatula to finish off the mixing by hand, scraping the bottom and sides of the bowl and folding the dough until the flour is incorporated. Add the crystallized ginger and continue folding with the spatula until it's evenly distributed.

5. Place the demerara sugar in a small bowl and set the baking sheets next to it to create an assembly line. Use a tablespoon to scoop a heaping mound of the dough and roll it between your palms into a 1½-inch ball (you can also use a ¾-ounce scoop). Dip half the

RECIPE CONTINUES

ball into the demerara sugar and place the ball sugar side up on the baking sheet. Repeat with the remaining dough, spacing the balls 2 inches apart.

6. Bake one sheet of cookies until the tops are cracked and there's a strong aroma of ginger wafting through your kitchen, 10 to 12 minutes. Repeat for the remaining sheet of cookies. Cool the cookies at least 10 minutes on the baking sheet before serving.

storage These cookies are irresistible straight from the oven or within the first day of baking; the cooled cookies can be stored in an airtight container for up to 3 days.

The Collapse
of Cookie Week

The four walls were somehow erect—held together only with royal icing. A batch of raw gingerbread dough lay in the trash (I forgot to add the sugar). I still had the roof to assemble on my "Gingerbread Brownstone," a replica of my upper Manhattan dwelling. The fire escape that I piped on with black royal icing hadn't quite set before I stood it up to create the structure. Black icing dripped down the gingerbread wall, as if the actual fire escape was melting from the blazing imaginary fire inside.

By this time, multiple cameramen started to surround me. It was week four of the show, and I had figured out by then that if the camera operators and producers surrounded your workstation, it was because something was going terribly wrong. I had a sneaking suspicion that my simple structure would not be able to sustain the weight of the roof that I hadn't yet placed on top, nor the criticism of the judges. Ayesha Curry and Spice Adams, standing at the front of the tent, shouted in unison: "Bakers, 5 minutes!"

There was no time left to figure out a work-around, so I gingerly placed the slab of gingerbread roof on top of the structure. It wobbled. I inched my hands away from the structure, and within what felt like seconds, the back wall collapsed in two!

Cameramen captured every angle of this cookie debacle. As if on cue, hot tears poured down my face. I cried silently. But I refused to collapse like my gingerbread brownstone. Through waterlogged eyes and blurred vision, I whipped up a quick batch of royal icing and glued the two pieces together in a Hail Mary attempt to fix the broken wall. Gobs of royal icing crept up the sides of the structure and dripped from the roof to resemble icicles. There were only two minutes left. I drenched the scene in a blizzard of frosting and finished it off with a heavy dusting of confectioners' sugar. The stoop slid down, as it was inadequately attached to the structure. I scurried to quickly reattach it. That heavy dusting of sugar made it so the cookies could no longer stand up on my winterscape. The snow rendered the icing-glue useless. Eventually, I wised up and used my finger to quickly shovel the confectioners'-sugar snow, which enabled the icing to be a sufficient adhesive to get my stoop reattached.

"10, 9, 8, . . . " The faster I scrambled, the more quickly tears slid down my face. " . . . 3, 2, 1—stop! Hands up, bakers!"

I dropped the piping bag full of frosting and raised my hands, unsure if it was in defeat or simply following directions.

When it came time for judging, I carefully brought my structure to the judges with the bravest face I could muster. It didn't take long for the criticism (and more tears) to flow. My dilapidated brownstone spoke for itself, even though some of the details like the imprint of bricks on the wall, and the glowing yellow windows to indicate the warmth of home, were still intact. The judges used a large, dramatic knife and cut the house in two and tasted it. They loved it!

I returned to my seat, and Paul Hollywood, in a rare display of affection, came to my station and gave me a small hug and words of encouragement. I couldn't help but smile.

Elimination that week proved to be the most contested yet. But despite my gingerbread debacle, I survived. The only sense I could make of this close call was: this will make for a *great* storyline, since everyone loves a comeback kid.

Sugar Cookie Cutouts

MAKES 2 TO 5 DOZEN, DEPENDING ON SIZE

There's something special about the buttery simplicity of these thin, soft cookies that are as versatile as the flavors that can be added, from vanilla extract to orange blossom water. I've tinkered with many sugar cookies over the years, and this one is my favorite. It's a rolled cookie, so you'll have to use your rolling pin (see my cookie tips, page 108). The dough is perfect for using different types of cookie cutters.

3 cups (375g) **all-purpose flour,** plus extra for rolling

½ teaspoon **kosher salt**

1 cup (2 sticks/226g) **unsalted butter,** room temperature

1 cup (200g) **granulated sugar**

1 large **egg,** room temperature

1 teaspoon **vanilla extract**

1. Add the flour to a large bowl. Whisk in the salt.

2. In the bowl of a stand mixer fitted with the paddle attachment, cream the butter and sugar on medium speed until the mixture becomes fluffy, very pale, and looks glossy like frosting, 4 to 5 minutes. Scrape the bottom and sides of the bowl as needed.

3. Add the egg and vanilla and keep beating on medium speed until everything is thoroughly incorporated, about 1 more minute. Reduce the speed to low and add the dry mixture a heaping spoonful at a time. The dough will initially appear scraggly. Keep mixing on low speed until the dough starts to come together in clumps and feels like Play-Doh, 45 to 60 seconds more—be careful not to overmix. If there is still flour remaining at the bottom of the bowl, use a large, sturdy rubber spatula to fold the flour into this stiff dough.

4. Tip the dough out onto a lightly floured work surface and divide it into 2 mounds. Roll one heap of dough between two 14-inch-long pieces of parchment or wax paper to about a 10 by 10-inch square that is about ¼ inch thick. Slide the paper-sandwiched dough onto a baking sheet and refrigerate until the dough is firm, about 30 minutes. Repeat with the other mass of dough.

5. Remove the first sheet of dough from the refrigerator. Remove one piece of parchment and use a cookie cutter to stamp out as many cookies as close together as possible. Line the baking sheet with parchment and use a spatula to transfer the cookies to the baking sheet, spacing them 2 inches apart (these cookies maintain their shape and don't spread). Reroll the scraps and cut out more cookies. Place the baking sheet in the fridge while you repeat the process with the second half of the dough.

6. Preheat the oven to 350°F and place a rack in the middle of the oven.

7. Place one of the baking sheets in the oven and bake until the cookies are cooked through and appear dry around the edges, 10 to 12 minutes. Let the cookies cool on the baking sheet for 10 minutes, then gently slide the parchment and cookies onto a cooling rack and let cool completely. Repeat with the remaining baking sheet of cookies. Serve.

Olive Oil–Chocolate Chunk Cookies

MAKES 1½ DOZEN COOKIES

A good chocolate chip cookie isn't just about taste—it's also about texture. The combination of both olive oil and butter in this cookie yields a buttery, delicious cookie with a texture that's the best of both worlds: crispy edges and a chewy center. This is my upgraded version of a chocolate chip cookie, and the results are Insta-worthy and dizzyingly appetizing cookies.

1½ cups (185g) **all-purpose flour**

½ teaspoon **baking powder**

½ teaspoon **baking soda**

½ teaspoon **kosher salt**

⅓ cup (80ml) **extra-virgin olive oil**

3 tablespoons (45g) **unsalted butter,** room temperature

¾ cup (150g) packed **light** or **dark brown sugar**

¼ cup (50g) **granulated sugar**

1 large **egg,** room temperature

1 teaspoon **vanilla extract**

6 ounces **semisweet** or **bittersweet chocolate** (chips or ½-inch chunks)

Flaky sea salt (optional)

1. Preheat the oven to 350°F and place a rack in the center of the oven. Line 2 baking pans with parchment paper and set aside.

2. In a large bowl, whisk the flour, baking powder, baking soda, and kosher salt together. Set aside.

3. Combine the olive oil, butter, brown sugar, and granulated sugar in the bowl of a stand mixer fitted with the paddle attachment. Mix on medium speed until combined, about 3 minutes. Once homogeneous, reduce the speed to low and add the egg and vanilla. Mix until combined.

4. Add the dry ingredients to the mixer and mix on low speed until just combined. Add the chocolate chips and mix for a couple of seconds. Remove the bowl and finish combining with a wooden spoon or a sturdy spatula.

5. Form 18 balls of dough, about 40 grams— a heaping 2 tablespoons—each. Place 9 balls of dough on each sheet. Bake until browned and set around the edges, 12 to 15 minutes. Remove from the oven and let cool slightly on a cooling rack before serving. Sprinkle with flaky sea salt, if desired.

storage These are best within the first 2 days, though they can be stored in an airtight container for up to 1 week, or the dough may be frozen in balls in a sealed freezer bag for up to 2 months. They can be baked frozen.

Cook the syrup until the mixture bubbles and reaches 244°F.

Pour the syrup into the egg whites by setting the pot along the lip of the bowl and drizzling in the syrup.

Continue to whisk on high for 1 minute.

Whisk on medium until the mixture cools slightly and the mixing bowl isn't hot to the touch, 4 to 5 minutes.

Lighten Up!
Making Meringue

Once you master making meringue, a myriad of desserts and cakes will be at your disposal, from marshmallows to macarons. A meringue is nothing more than egg whites beaten with sugar to varying degrees of stiffness. You can use meringue in a buttercream to make the frosting extra light and airy, mix it with almond flour to pipe macarons (see page 91), or employ it as a leavening agent in soufflés (see page 79) and chiffon cakes (see page 189). You can even bake the meringue all by itself in a low oven, turning it into a cookie (a meringue!).

There are three types of meringues: French, Italian, and Swiss. I prefer French and Italian meringues because they are less dense, so those are the two styles I make the most. The difference between them lies in how the sugar is incorporated.

French meringue is the simplest (and most common) to make. You just whip egg whites until soft peaks form, then sprinkle in granulated sugar and continue to whip until the meringue is stiff and glossy. While it's the easiest, French meringue is also the least stable. It's perfect for folding into soufflés and chiffon cake batter, but it's trickier for those desserts where you want it to hold its shape, like piped buttercream decorations or the topping of a lemon meringue pie.

When you incorporate French meringue into a batter, add one-fourth of the meringue at first and give it a good stir, which will loosen the batter. Then, use a rubber spatula to fold in the rest of the meringue, scooping under and over the batter while also rotating the bowl. Continue to fold just until no streaks of meringue remain. If you overmix the meringue, you risk deflating it, and your soufflés, chiffon cakes, and macarons won't rise as tall.

Italian meringue is a little more advanced, since you have to cook the sugar to 244°F (a thermometer is most helpful) before adding it to the egg whites (see opposite page). It's the most stable, although it can be a little intimidating for novice bakers.

Just remember to lighten up. The word *meringue* may be intimidating, but the wondrous desserts that it enlightens are endless!

See page 27 for video tutorial instructions on making meringue.

Chocolate Mint Moon Pies

MAKES 1½ DOZEN SANDWICH COOKIES

"Throw me somethin', mista!" is the rallying cry of Mardi Gras revelers—a plea for plastic beads, cups, and doubloons. And if you're really lucky, you might even catch a MoonPie (no space!). These beloved little individually wrapped pastries tossed from Mardi Gras floats were one of my favorite throws at parades. It wasn't until I was older that I realized I could get them year-round at convenience stores.

Making these cookies sandwiched with the creamy marshmallow and dipped in chocolate is as much fun as it is to catch them at a parade. The Wilton Dark Cocoa Mint Candy Melts are at party supply stores or online; I use them here because candy melts are easier than melted chocolate for dipping to get a thin layer of coating, but melted chocolate also works.

MARSHMALLOW CREAM FILLING

¼ cup (60ml) **cold water**

2 (¼-ounce/7g) packages **unflavored gelatin powder**

6 large **egg whites**

2 cups (400g) **granulated sugar**

6 tablespoons (120g) **corn syrup**

1 cup (240ml) **water**

1 teaspoon **vanilla extract**

MOON PIES

2 batches **Chocolate Shortbread Cookies** (page 110), made with 3-inch fluted-edge cutter

2 (12-ounce) packages **Wilton Dark Cocoa Mint Candy Melts** (or other chocolate or candy melt)

½ cup (60ml) **vegetable** or **coconut oil**

1. Prepare the marshmallow cream filling: Place the cold water in a small bowl and sprinkle the gelatin over the top. Use a fork to combine as soon as the powder hits the water so that it doesn't clump. The gelatin will absorb the water and gel quickly.

2. In the bowl of a stand mixer fitted with the whisk attachment, start whisking the egg whites on low speed.

3. Add the sugar, corn syrup, and water to a small saucepan. Cook over medium heat until the syrup reaches 241°F on a digital thermometer, about 15 minutes. (After about 5 minutes, you will see thousands of tiny bubbles simmering under the surface of the water. Keep cooking. At 6 minutes, bubbles will start dancing around and at 7 minutes, they begin to make their way to the center of the pan. The syrup will start bubbling more aggressively, and the tiny bubbles that were trapped underneath will break their way to the surface. By 10 minutes, the bubbles will be only on the surface, and eventually, they will take longer and longer to pop. By 15 minutes, there will be bubbles all over, some big and some small, and some defiantly holding their shape.) At this point, crank up the speed on the mixer to high. The egg whites should be just starting to form peaks as the sugar syrup reaches 244°F.

4. While the sugar is cooking, scoop the gelatin into a small saucepan. Heat on the lowest setting just until the gelatin melts, which happens quickly. Pour the hot syrup

RECIPE CONTINUES

into the whipping egg whites by setting the pot just along the lip of the bowl and drizzling the hot sugar on the side of the bowl so that it doesn't splash. Pour in the melted gelatin (if it has again solidified, just stick it back on the stove on the lowest setting until it melts) and continue to whisk on high speed for 1 minute. Add the vanilla. Reduce the speed to medium and continue to whisk until the mixture cools slightly so that the mixing bowl isn't hot to the touch, 4 to 5 minutes.

5. Immediately transfer the marshmallow filling to a piping bag fitted with a large tip (such as Wilton 2A) to prevent it from setting. (If you don't have a piping bag, no problem— you can fill the cookies using a spoon.)

6. Make the moon pies: Set half the cookies on your work surface. Pipe or spoon a mound of filling (about 2 tablespoons) onto the flat-side of the center of these cookies. Let the cookies sit undisturbed for 15 minutes so the filling starts to set. Place a second cookie, flat-side down, on top of the filling (don't press—the weight of the cookie is enough to sandwich it). Let the cookies sit at room temperature for 3 hours.

7. Melt the candy melts according to the package directions, being careful not to overheat, which will ruin the silky texture of the chocolate. When the chocolate is melted, stir in the oil.

8. Place the filled cookies on a cooling rack with a tray underneath to catch drips. Dip the cookies in the melted chocolate or spoon the melted chocolate over the top of the cookies and use the back of the spoon to coax it down the sides. Continue until all the moon pies are coated. Let the chocolate set completely, about 30 minutes. Remove the moon pies from the rack with an offset spatula or butter knife and enjoy.

---

storage Store in an airtight container, separated by parchment paper so that they don't stick together, for up to 1 week.

VARIATION

Banana Cream Moon Pies
Make the filling according to the directions. When adding the vanilla, also add ¼ teaspoon banana cream extract (see Note). Use one batch of Sugar Cookie Cutouts (page 121) instead of the chocolate cookies and use 2 (12-ounce) packages of Wilton Yellow Candy Melts in place of the chocolate. Proceed with the recipe as instructed.

---

note Banana cream extract is super concentrated, four times more powerful than most other extracts. If substituting banana liqueur, use 1 tablespoon; if substituting with regular-strength banana extract, use 1 teaspoon.

Italian
"Pot" Brownies

Growing up in the '90s had its simplicities. Satisfying a brownie craving was as easy as putting a box of brownie mix in the grocery cart and deciding between "3 eggs for cake-like brownies" and "2 eggs for fudge-y brownies." (The answer was *always* 2 eggs for fudge-y brownies.)

We would top the box-mix brownies with a scoop of Blue Bell's French Vanilla ice cream. The ice cream pierced the warm and chewy brownies and was a total celebration of polar opposites: in flavor (chocolate and vanilla), in temperature (hot and cold), and in texture (chewy and creamy). This emphasis on contrasts proved to be an early lesson in how to construct a winning dessert.

When I studied abroad in Paris, I quickly learned that box brownies were an American invention and that it wasn't chic enough for the *marchés* and *épiceries* in the City of Light. During spring break, I traveled to Florence to meet up with Grace, a lifelong friend, who was spending a semester abroad in Italy. We were each months into our semesters abroad; Grace was making panna cotta in Italy (her instructor said the panna cotta should "shake like a woman's bosom"), and I was intoxicated by rosés from the Loire Valley and croissants from the neighborhood boulangerie. But even when you're immersed in the most gourmet of food lands, sometimes what you want most is a taste of home.

So, we did what any mildly homesick American college students might have done—we made brownies. We didn't have brownie mix; we didn't even have a pan! Grace's scarcely furnished kitchen did contain, however, a single pot. We made the brownies entirely in the pot and whisked them together with a fork. We even *baked* them in the pot, which worked surprisingly well, earning these brownies the cheeky name "pot brownies." (We topped them with vanilla gelato because we were in Italy, after all.)

I have since come to my senses and have stopped buying box mixes. Brownies have been added to my just-as-easy-to-make-from-scratch, one-bowl (or one-pot) list, because where there's a whisk, there's a way—and when there isn't a whisk, or even a pan, there's usually a fork and a pot!

Dark Chocolate Sea Salt Brownies

MAKES 1 DOZEN BROWNIES

These brownies have a glossy, crackling top and rich, fudge-y centers. They're thick, but still have a lightness to them that makes them impossible to stop eating. Cut them large, or you'll definitely go back for seconds. The chocolate is the star, so now's a good time to splurge on the good stuff (it really does make a difference!). I like Guittard 60% or 70% cacao dark chocolate, but I have also made these with the supermarket brand of dark chocolate and they were still the *belle of the bake sale*. Coffee enhances the flavor of the chocolate, but it's okay if you choose to leave it out. This recipe uses all chocolate and no cocoa powder, which is great for getting that dense, fudge-like texture. They are super moist—to make them easier to cut (if you can stand to wait), let them cool completely before cutting them.

---

8 ounces **dark chocolate,** finely chopped

1 cup (2 sticks/226g) **unsalted butter,** cut into 1-inch pieces

1 teaspoon **kosher salt**

1 tablespoon (6g) **instant coffee powder** or **brewed coffee** (optional)

2 teaspoons **vanilla extract**

5 large **eggs**

1 cup (200g) **granulated sugar**

1 cup (200g) packed **light** or **dark brown sugar**

1 cup (125g) **all-purpose flour**

½ teaspoon **flaky sea salt**

1. Preheat the oven to 350°F and place a rack in the middle of the oven. Line a 9 by 13-inch metal baking pan with parchment paper, leaving some paper to overhang the edges to easily lift out the brownies.

2. Place the chocolate in a large, heatproof bowl along with the butter. Add 2 inches of water to a pot and bring it to a simmer over high heat. Reduce the heat to low and place the bowl on top (making sure the bottom of the bowl doesn't touch the simmering water; otherwise the chocolate might "burn" and the texture will become grainy instead of melting into a smooth emulsion) and stir occasionally with a rubber spatula until melted. Make sure the water from the pot doesn't boil.

3. Remove the bowl from the pot and turn off the heat. Stir in the kosher salt, instant coffee, and vanilla.

4. In a large bowl, whisk the eggs and sugars together until completely combined. If the brown sugar has any large lumps, use your fingers or the back of a spoon to break them up. Add the chocolate-butter mixture and whisk until just combined. Place a sieve over the bowl and sift in the flour. Use a large rubber spatula to fold in the flour until no streaks remain. Pour the brownie batter into the pan, using the spatula to spread it out evenly. (The batter is pretty liquidy and thinner than a typical cake batter.)

RECIPE CONTINUES

5. Bake until a toothpick inserted into the center only has a few stubborn crumbs clinging to it, 25 to 30 minutes. Remove from the oven and immediately sprinkle with flaky sea salt. Set on a cooling rack for at least 15 minutes, then use the overhanging parchment to lift the brownies out of the pan. Cut into squares just before serving.

storage The brownies will keep for up to 1 week, covered, at room temperature.

Thicky-Thick Peanut Butter Brownies

A cake-like mixture of peanut butter, eggs, and flour punctuates the brownie batter, resulting in deep pockets of peanut butter goodness speckled throughout. To make the peanut butter swirl, use a fork to combine 1 cup (240g) peanut butter, ½ cup (100g) granulated sugar, 2 large eggs, and ½ teaspoon kosher salt in a small bowl. Prepare the brownie batter as instructed through step 4. Then, over the brownie batter in the pan, dollop the peanut butter mixture by the spoonful in a checkerboard-like manner. Use a small spoon or butter knife to drag lines across the batter to lightly break up the peanut butter. It won't swirl or mix completely and that's okay. The goal is to have big chunky pockets of peanut butter. Bake, 25 to 30 minutes, or until a toothpick inserted into the center comes out with only a crumb or two attached. Cool and slice as instructed.

COBBLERS,

PIES & TARTS

If pie crust were a person, I'd want to be her. "Relax and chill" is her mantra, but she doesn't shrink away when things heat up. She'd teach me the importance of rest and show me that sometimes you've got to take care of yourself so you're ready when times get tough. In fact, she's *made for the heat.* That's because some of the hottest ovens we find ourselves in are just what we need to create the steam that's necessary to be our best, layered selves. And it's okay when things don't go as planned; you can always patch the ripped dough—or a broken heart or a shattered dream—back together.

Picnic Peach Cobbler

MAKES ONE 8-INCH COBBLER

Peach cobbler is a late-summer dish that in my experience is most enjoyed at church picnics and family reunions. It holds rare company with potato salad and macaroni and cheese in that it's so beloved that it's met with both adulation and scrutiny. Once a peach cobbler is spotted at the end of a serving line, the conversation among people goes a little something like this: "Ooh, a peach cobbler!," followed by, "Do you know who made it?" The second question is asked with a heavy dose of skepticism to balance the excitement, as if the peach cobbler would be too much of a letdown if it wasn't made by the right person.

It's a brave soul who chooses to bless these gatherings with a peach cobbler that will bring out the harshest critic in even the sweetest, hat-wearing, peppermint-wielding church ladies and aunties. Before taking that first bite, you might hear someone asking the person seated next to them, "So . . . how was it?" They peer into their neighbor's plate, looking for signs of a well-made cobbler: lots of crust, thick syrup, chunky peaches.

Fear not—this recipe has you covered! The ratio of crust to filling is just right—lots (and lots!) of crust, but enough juicy peaches to balance each bite. The orange zest, lemon juice, and brandy add an extra punch of flavor, bringing out the sweet yet tart nectar in the peaches. If you bake the cobbler long enough and let it rest, the pie dough–like crust in this cobbler won't be soupy (many Southerners prefer pie crust to biscuit dough in our cobblers).

Juicy peaches? Yes! Juicy cobbler? No, thanks. The glossy finish from the egg wash will make the rays of sunshine on an outdoor picnic look like light refracting on the facets of a diamond. The onlookers won't be able to resist digging into this gem.

make ahead You can make the cobbler through step 6 and then freeze it for up to 2 months. If freezing, double-wrap it in plastic wrap. When you're ready to bake, start at step 7. Since it's frozen, increase the baking time by a few minutes.

---

2 disks of dough for Flaky Pie Crust (page 140), or 2 store-bought pie crust rounds

1 tablespoon all-purpose flour, plus extra for rolling

8 large or 10 medium (about 4 pounds) ripe peaches, peeled (3 pounds frozen peach wedges, defrosted and drained, may also be used)

¾ cup (150g) granulated sugar, plus more for sprinkling

¼ cup (30g) cornstarch

¾ teaspoon ground nutmeg

1 teaspoon kosher salt

1 tablespoon (15ml) fresh lemon juice (from 1 lemon)

1 teaspoon grated orange zest

1 tablespoon (15ml) brandy

2 teaspoons vanilla extract

4 tablespoons (55g) cold unsalted butter, cut into ½-inch pieces

1 large egg

Ground cinnamon

---

1. Roll two-thirds of the dough into a 12-inch square on a lightly floured surface or between 2 pieces of wax paper (you'll need

RECIPE CONTINUES

one disk plus a portion of the other disk). Fit the dough into the corners and up the sides of an 8-inch square baking pan and refrigerate while preparing the filling (about 20 minutes). Roll the remaining dough into an 8-inch square on a lightly floured surface or between 2 pieces of wax paper. Place the square of dough on a baking sheet and refrigerate it while you prepare the filling.

2. Halve and pit each peach and then cut into ¾-inch wedges. Place the wedges in a large bowl with the sugar, cornstarch, nutmeg, salt, lemon juice, orange zest, brandy, and vanilla. Mix well using a large spoon until the ingredients evenly coat the peaches.

3. Remove the dough-lined baking pan from the refrigerator and sprinkle the bottom with 1 tablespoon sugar and 1 tablespoon flour in an even layer. Arrange the peach wedges in the pan. Be sure to pour any accumulated juices over the top. Add the butter pieces over the peaches.

4. Remove the square piece of dough from the refrigerator. Place it over the peaches, pinching the edges of the 2 doughs to seal.

5. Make a 2-inch X in the middle of the top of the dough, and eight 2-inch slits around the center X. It's important that the slits are large enough to vent the steam that forms as the cobbler bakes. (If the steam can't evaporate, the cobbler will be soupy!)

6. Place the cobbler in the freezer for at least 20 minutes (the longer it freezes, the colder the butter becomes and the flakier the crust will be!). If it freezes completely, that's just fine—it'll just need a little more time to bake.

7. Preheat the oven to 400°F and place a rack in the middle of the oven. Prepare the egg wash by whisking the egg in a small bowl. Remove the cobbler from the freezer and use a pastry brush to brush the egg wash evenly over the top (in a pinch, I use a paper towel to dab and spread the egg wash). Sprinkle a generous amount of granulated sugar and ground cinnamon on top of the crust.

8. Bake the cobbler for 15 minutes, then reduce the heat to 350°F and bake until the juices are aggressively bubbling up through the vents, even in the center of the cobbler, an additional 50 to 60 minutes. Let cool slightly, then enjoy. Who can resist a peach cobbler warm from the oven? Not me! If you are enjoying this at home, do yourself a favor and eat it warm with a scoop of ice cream.

storage If you're taking the cobbler to a picnic or having it later, allow it to cool on a cooling rack until room temperature, which will help the filling set. Once completely cooled, store it covered in the fridge for up to 3 days.

Letting Off Steam!

Always let your baked goods cool to room temperature before you wrap them and put them away. By letting baked goods cool completely, you're letting the steam escape. And it's better that the steam escapes into the atmosphere than clinging to the top of plastic wrap or the lid of a plastic container, which will make your baked goods soggy.

Flaky Pie Crust

MAKES DOUGH FOR 2 SINGLE-CRUST PIES OR 1 DOUBLE-CRUST PIE

If there's one pie crust recipe you need to master, it's this one. It's easy to roll out, bakes up flaky, and is buttery-delicious. Before I knew better, I spent the better part of a decade making pie dough in a stand mixer. I let the machine do all the work, and I mixed until it was a giant clump of sticky dough. This overhandling of the dough caused the crust to be tough and to shrink in the oven. I finally wised up and started giving pie dough the respect and delicate handling she deserves.

I tested all my favorite pie doughs to come up with this recipe, from Grandma's that uses egg yolks (and lard!), to my mom's go-to that uses vegetable shortening. And I tested many more with ingredients varying wildly, from vodka to baking powder and with cream cheese or heavy cream. I settled on a recipe that's all about flavor (butter and *only* butter). A couple teaspoons of sugar help with browning, and the apple cider vinegar adds some tang while making the dough just a tad harder to be overworked.

Note that this recipe gives you an unbaked crust. Intended use determines whether you will want to bake the crust before filling. See page 173 for tips on either partially or fully baking the crust before filling it and page 174 for ideas on how to use this dough and what fillings it works best with.

2½ cups (300g) **all-purpose flour**

2 teaspoons **granulated sugar**

1 teaspoon **kosher salt**

1 cup (2 sticks/226g) cold **unsalted butter,** cut into 1-inch slices

⅓ cup (80ml) **ice cold water,** or more as needed

2 tablespoons (30ml) **apple cider vinegar**

1. Add the flour, sugar, and salt to the bowl of a food processor, or a large bowl if using a pastry blender. Pulse or whisk until the mixture is combined.

2. Add the butter and pulse until most of the butter is broken into pea-size pieces, about 15 pulses. There will be some larger pieces of butter, and that's a good thing. If using a pastry blender, blend the butter until it's pea size.

3. Add the cold water and vinegar to a cup and pour the liquid over the crumbly flour-butter mixture. Pulse until it looks like tiny clumps (like space dots ice cream), and there are no large pockets of flour. If using a pastry blender, use a large rubber spatula for this step, folding until no large pockets of flour remain.

4. Tip the mixture onto your work surface and use a light touch to gather the dough together and pat it down until it's about 1 inch thick. Fold the dough in half, then pat it back down to a 1-inch block. Repeat twice, then pat and gather the dough into 2 round disks, smoothing the sides so they aren't dry and crumbly. Wrap the disks tightly in plastic and let them rest in the refrigerator for at least 30 minutes, and up to 3 days.

storage The dough can be frozen for up to 1 month and defrosted in the refrigerator between 1 and 3 days.

How to Make the Flakiest Pie Crust

Everyone wants flaky pie crust! Here is how I achieve all those layers:

1. HANDLE LESS FOR A TENDER CRUST. The butter should be quickly and efficiently "cut into" the flour. By moving quickly, the butter stays solid, which creates steam when in the hot oven, yielding flaky layers. You can cut the butter into the flour by pulsing in a food processor or with a handheld pastry blender (a stand mixer can get the job done in a pinch—just don't overdo the mixing).

2. ADD JUST ENOUGH WATER. If you grab a handful of the finished dough and squeeze it in your fist, it should clump together without breaking into sandy bits when you let go. This is how you know that you've added enough water. Adding too much water will cause your dough to be sticky, resulting in a tough crust.

3. CLUMP AND FOLD FOR LOADS OF LAYERS. After I know the dough has enough water to hold together, I turn it out onto my work surface. The dough will look shaggy, but that's okay because it's time to clump it! By gathering the bits, pressing them together, and folding, you create the layers before the dough goes in the oven. After clumping, press the dough about 1 inch thick and then fold it in half on top of itself. Folding is an easy way to create even more layers. I repeat this step three times for maximum flaky layers.

4. RELAX AND CHILL. Now you have what looks like pie dough! The next step is super important, so don't skip it. You get to take a break while the dough chills in the fridge—at least 30 minutes. By resting, the liquid in the dough has a chance to hydrate the flour, then the gluten in the flour relaxes—making the dough easier to roll out.

5. ROLL THE DOUGH. Roll the dough out on a lightly floured surface, or between 2 sheets of wax paper, to a ¼- to ⅛-inch thickness. The trick to ensuring your crust is rolled in an even layer is to use rolling pin rings—a low-tech, high-functioning contraption that ensures an even thickness.

6. TRANSFER THE DOUGH TO THE PAN. If your dough is between 2 pieces of wax paper, peel the top layer away and flip the remaining layer onto the pie dish before peeling the second layer off. Press the dough into the pie plate, then transfer to the refrigerator or freezer and take another break! (If it's going into the freezer, 20 minutes is sufficient, or chill for at least 30 minutes in the fridge.) The second rest allows the gluten in the flour to further relax, preventing the pie crust from shrinking during baking.

Peach Crisp

MAKES ONE 8- OR 9-INCH CRISP

Crisps are a flavorful and satisfying alternative for people who want the same peachy goodness of a cobbler or pie but don't want to fool around with pie dough. You can peel the peaches if you like, but I keep the skin on because it fits the rustic nature of the dish and it makes the prep easier! For a gluten-free version, use rolled oats instead of all-purpose flour. This can be prepared in a pie dish or square baking pan.

CRISP TOPPING

½ cup (60g) all-purpose flour or old-fashioned rolled oats

½ cup (50g) almond flour

½ cup (100g) packed light or dark brown sugar

1 teaspoon kosher salt

5 tablespoons (70g) unsalted butter, melted

PEACH FILLING

4 large or 5 medium peaches
(about 2½ pounds), halved and pitted

⅓ cup (65g) packed light or dark brown sugar

3 tablespoons (25g) all-purpose flour or cornstarch

2 tablespoons (30ml) fresh lemon juice

1 tablespoon (15ml) brandy (optional)

1 teaspoon grated orange zest

1 teaspoon vanilla extract

½ teaspoon ground nutmeg

½ cup (60g) roughly chopped pecans

storage If not enjoying immediately, let the crisp rest at room temperature to firm up before storing, covered, in the refrigerator for up to 3 days.

1. Preheat the oven to 350°F and place a rack in the middle of the oven.

2. Make the crisp topping: Combine the flours, brown sugar, and salt in a small bowl. Use a fork to combine. Pour in the melted butter and then gently stir with a fork until clumps form and all the flour is moistened. Large clumps are okay—you can break them up once the topping has had some time to freeze. Place the bowl in the freezer so the butter can firm up while preparing the filling.

3. Prepare the peach filling: Cut the halved peaches in half, then each piece into thirds. Place the peaches in a large bowl and add the brown sugar, flour, lemon juice, brandy (if using), orange zest, vanilla, and nutmeg. Toss until all the ingredients evenly coat the peaches.

4. Transfer the peaches and any accumulated juices to an 8- or 9-inch baking pan or pie dish. Sprinkle the chopped pecans on top.

5. Remove the crisp topping from the freezer. Use a fork or your fingertips to break up any clumps that are larger than a garbanzo bean. Sprinkle the crisp topping on top of the peach wedges in an even layer.

6. Bake until the crisp is browned on top, you can hear the peach juices sizzling, and a fork easily slides into a peach wedge, 1 hour to 1 hour 5 minutes. Remove from the oven and enjoy straight away for a warm, satisfying treat.

RECIPE CONTINUES

Apple Crisp

Make the same topping. Replace the peaches with
6 large, firm apples (such as Granny Smith), about
2½ pounds, peeled, cored, and sliced into ¾-inch
wedges. Replace the orange zest, nutmeg, brandy, and
pecans with ½ teaspoon ground cinnamon. Bake the
crisp as instructed.

Blueberry Crisp

Make the same topping. Replace the peaches with
4½ cups fresh or frozen blueberries. Increase the flour
or cornstarch to ¼ cup. Eliminate the brandy, orange
zest, nutmeg, and pecans. Bake the crisp as instructed.

Rhubarb-Strawberry Crisp

Make the same topping. Replace the peaches with
4 cups thinly sliced rhubarb (about 1½ pounds) and
3 cups hulled and sliced fresh strawberries (about
1 pound). Increase the brown sugar to ½ cup and the
flour or cornstarch to ¼ cup. Eliminate the brandy,
orange zest, nutmeg, and pecans. Bake the crisp as
instructed.

The Case for Store-Bought Pie Dough

Here's a bit of baker's blasphemy: you don't have to make your own crust! I'm a believer in ready-made pie crusts and here's why. Store-bought pie doughs cut down on prep time, and a lot of them are pretty tasty. The only type of crust I buy is the pre-rolled "fit them in the pan" rounds of dough. They're a near-perfect replacement for flaky pie dough, such as you'd use in an apple pie or a peach cobbler. Also, unlike the crusts that are fitted into disposable foil pans, you can actually roll these with a rolling pin to expand their size for a deep-dish pie plate or use them as a top crust on a double-crust pie.

This pie dough can be purchased frozen or refrigerated. I prefer refrigerated so that I don't have to worry about defrosting it when I need it. Just be sure to set it out at room temperature for about 10 minutes before unrolling; otherwise, the dough will crack and tear as you try to unroll it. If it does tear, don't worry—just patch it back together! Once the dough round is unrolled, you can fit it into your pie plate. At this point, set the pie back in the fridge to firm up, just as you'd do for a homemade crust. You can even blind-bake the crust. Just keep an eye on it because it may bake more quickly than your homemade version!

One-Bowl Blueberry Buckle

MAKES ONE 9-INCH BUCKLE

During the summer before my senior year of high school, my friends and I would wake up early every Saturday in June to pick blueberries. As we drove to the blueberry farm in East Feliciana Parish, familiar suburban fixtures melted into endless rural landscapes under the Louisiana sun. Armed with a repurposed gallon milk jug with its top cut off, which I tethered to my denim short-all's belt loop, we'd head into the fields in search of the plumpest blueberries. I reached both hands high over my head to pluck blueberries so dark they were ashy. I always filled my belly before the makeshift bucket.

One of my oldest friends, Grace Hinton, shared this recipe with me after one morning of blueberry picking. I have since made this one-bowl buckle countless times. The admirers of this crave-worthy dish either love it or *learn* to love it. If you're not swooning the first time you try it, the buttery and caramelized edges of the cake that rise over the plump, juicy berries will have you hooked by the second time. Be sure to serve it with a scoop of vanilla ice cream—the perfect creamy, cold complement to the syrupy, warm berries.

1. Preheat the oven to 375°F and place a rack in the middle of the oven. Place the butter in a 9 by 5-inch loaf pan and put it in the hot oven. When the butter has melted, remove the pan from the oven.

2. Meanwhile, whisk together the flour, sugar, milk, and salt in a large bowl (it's okay if the batter is a little lumpy). Pour the batter into the pan with the melted butter and use a spoon to lightly mix it. There should be visible streaks of melted butter that don't get completely mixed; this yields the buttery, caramelized edges.

3. Place the blueberries on top of the batter in an even layer. Bake until the top is golden brown all over, 50 to 60 minutes. (If you remove it too early, the buckle will indeed "buckle" in the middle and fall—which would still be tasty, though sunken!) Wait until it's golden all over the top and set in the center. Place the buckle on a cooling rack for 10 minutes before serving warm with a scoop of ice cream.

½ cup (1 stick/113g) **unsalted butter**

1 cup (125g) **self-rising flour** (see Note)

1 cup (200g) **granulated sugar**

1 cup (240ml) **whole milk**

1 teaspoon **kosher salt**

1 cup (150g) fresh or frozen **blueberries**

Vanilla ice cream, for serving

note This recipe uses self-rising flour, a staple in most Southern pantries that contains leavening and salt. If you don't have any on hand, just add 1½ teaspoons baking powder and an additional ¼ teaspoon salt to the flour.

storage You can refrigerate the buckle, covered, for up to 3 days.

Double-Crust Apple Pie

MAKES 1 DEEP-DISH PIE

This apple pie may be one of my favorite desserts to both make *and* eat. As much as I love a homemade crust, this is one recipe where it's okay to skip it and go with the store-bought pie rounds. It's one of my favorite pies to bake when I'm not home because it comes together so easily, yet the taste surely impresses whomever you're baking for. Store-bought pie dough is really simple to cut into strips for a lattice top. You can visit foodieinnewyork.com/tutorials to watch a video and learn how! A scoop of vanilla ice cream pairs perfectly with a slice of this pie.

3 tablespoons (25g) **all-purpose flour**, plus extra for rolling

2 **store-bought rounds of pie dough**

6 **apples** (about 3 pounds), peeled, cored, and sliced into ½-inch-thick wedges (I like to use Granny Smith or McIntosh)

½ cup (100g) **granulated sugar**

1 teaspoon **ground cinnamon**

¼ teaspoon freshly **grated nutmeg**

1 tablespoon (15ml) **fresh lemon juice**

Dash of kosher **salt**

2 tablespoons (28g) **unsalted butter**, cut into ½-inch pieces

1 large **egg**

Demerara or more **granulated sugar**, for sprinkling

1. On a lightly floured surface, roll out one disk of pie dough into an 11-inch circle, and transfer it into a 9-inch pie plate. Fit the dough into the pie plate, trimming any edge overhang that's greater than 1 inch. Place the pie plate in the refrigerator while you roll the second piece of dough into a 10-inch circle.

Place the round of dough onto a baking sheet and refrigerate it to chill the butter.

2. In a large bowl, combine the apples, granulated sugar, 3 tablespoons flour, cinnamon, nutmeg, lemon juice, and salt. Use a large spoon or both hands to mix until all the apple wedges are evenly coated.

3. Transfer the apple mixture and any remaining juices to the crust. Scatter the butter pieces on top.

4. Remove the flat circle of dough from the refrigerator and lay it over the apples. Trim any overhang of dough that's longer than 1 inch and fold the rest of the dough under. Crimp and seal the edges of the crust using the tines of a fork. Place the pie in the freezer for 30 minutes.

5. Preheat the oven to 350°F and place a rack in the middle of the oven.

6. Crack the egg into a small bowl and whisk well. Remove the pie from the freezer. Using a pastry brush, brush the egg wash over the crust. Make a 2-inch *X* vent in the middle of the top crust, and eight 2-inch slits around the center *X*. It's important that your slits are large enough so steam can escape while the pie bakes. (This helps ensure your pie filling won't be soupy and that your crust stays crisp and flaky.)

7. Sprinkle the crust with the demerara sugar. Place the pie on a rimmed baking sheet and bake until the crust is golden and the juices in the center of the pie are bubbling up through the vents, 45 to 60 minutes. Remove the pie from the oven and cool for at least 1 hour before serving so the filling can firm up. Serve with ice cream, if desired.

Bourbon Pecan Pie

MAKES ONE 9-INCH PIE

When I was growing up in Louisiana, fall meant pecans littering the ground from the stately trees in our suburban neighborhood. On walks home from the bus stop, we would dip into various neighbors' backyards and gather as many pecans as would fit in our pockets and backpacks. My favorite thing to do once all the nuts had been shelled (by hand!) was to make pecan pie.

This recipe uses cane syrup, which adds a more complex sweetness than corn syrup. Plus, by toasting the pecans here, you bring out the bitter umami flavor, which balances the sweetness of the caramel-like filling. The heavy doses of vanilla and bourbon enhance the pecan flavor while also toning down the sweetness.

4 large **eggs**

4 tablespoons (55g) **unsalted butter**, melted and slightly cooled

1 tablespoon (8g) fine or medium grind **cornmeal**

1 tablespoon (15ml) **vanilla extract**

1 teaspoon **kosher salt**

1 cup **cane syrup** (340g), I use Steen's "100% Pure Cane Syrup" or Lyle's Golden Syrup "Cane Sugar Syrup"

½ cup (100g) **granulated sugar**

½ cup (100g) packed **light** or **dark brown sugar**

3 tablespoons (45ml) **bourbon**

2½ cups toasted **pecan halves**

1 disk of dough for **Flaky Pie Crust** (page 140), rolled out, fitted into a 9-inch pie plate, and partially baked (see page 173)

1. In a large bowl, whisk together the eggs, melted butter, cornmeal, vanilla, and salt.

2. Combine the cane syrup, sugars, and bourbon in a medium saucepan set over medium heat. Use a wooden spoon or whisk to stir continuously. When the syrup starts to boil, cook an additional 2 minutes, then remove the pan from the heat.

3. Use one hand to continuously whisk the egg mixture and use the other hand to slowly pour one-third of the hot syrup into the egg mixture. Continuously whisking tempers the eggs so they can be heated without scrambling. Pour the egg mixture into the saucepan with the syrup, continuing to whisk constantly. Stir in the pecans and set aside for 30 minutes to let the syrup mixture cool.

4. Preheat the oven to 325°F and place a rack in the middle of the oven.

5. When the syrup is at room temperature, pour it into the par-baked pie crust and bake until the center of the pie is just set and doesn't jiggle, 55 to 60 minutes. If the middle hasn't set but the pecans are browning, tent loosely with foil.

6. Remove the pie from the oven and let cool on a wire rack for at least 4 hours so the filling can firm up. Slice and serve.

storage This pie tastes even better the next day, so it's a great make-ahead recipe. The pie can be stored, covered, at room temperature for up to 3 days.

Candied Sweet Potato Pie

MAKES ONE 9-INCH PIE

Chances are, there's someone in your family who makes *the best* sweet potato pie. In my family, it's my mom. Hers is light and tender, and it captures all the goodness of candied yams without being too sweet. She uses evaporated milk—"pet milk," as she calls it (a reference to the first company to produce evaporated milk)—and adds sugar and spices until it tastes "just right." She always adds a little acid—orange juice or pineapple juice—to balance out the sweetness, and she uses both vanilla *and* almond extracts.

This recipe is inspired by my mom. And her recipe was inspired by my great-grandmother Lillie. My mom went to Grandma Lillie's house when she first married my dad, and my great-grandmother taught her how to make this pie. She gave her tips like these: *only make one pie crust at a time* (smaller batches were easier to handle before there were food processors), and *only use one egg.*

I upgraded the acid from a splash of juice to freshly grated orange zest, which really makes the flavor pop. I use Amaretto liqueur in place of almond extract and a little less sugar. I stick with the evaporated milk, which makes this pie lighter than one made with cream. The pecans add a nice crunch and also balance the sweetness. With this recipe, it just might be *you* who becomes the person in your family who makes *the best* sweet potato pie.

2 or 3 **sweet potatoes**, cooked, peeled and mashed (see page 155)

4 tablespoons (55g) **unsalted butter**, melted

½ cup (100g) **granulated sugar**

6 tablespoons (75g) firmly packed **light** or **dark brown sugar**

3 large **eggs**

1 cup (240ml) **evaporated milk**

2 tablespoons (30ml) **almond liqueur** or **orange liqueur** (optional)

1 tablespoon (15ml) **vanilla extract**

1 teaspoon **ground cinnamon**

¼ teaspoon freshly **grated nutmeg**

¼ teaspoon **ground ginger**

⅛ teaspoon **ground cloves**

½ teaspoon **kosher salt**

Grated zest from ¼ **orange**

½ cup (60g) toasted **pecans**, roughly chopped

1 disk of dough for **Flaky Pie Crust** (page 140), fitted into a 9-inch pie plate and partially baked (see page 173); or 1 **Graham Cracker Pie Crust** (page 171) in a 9-inch pie plate, baked; or 1 **store-bought 9-inch pie crust** in a pan, partially baked (see Note on page 154)

---

1. Preheat the oven to 350°F and set a rack in the middle of the oven.

2. Add 2 cups (510g) of mashed sweet potato and melted butter to a food processor and pulse 5 or 6 times until well combined. Don't overprocess the sweet potatoes, lest they become gummy. Use a rubber spatula to scrape the bottom of the food processor and

RECIPE CONTINUES

then add the sugars, eggs, evaporated milk, almond liqueur (if using), vanilla, cinnamon, nutmeg, ginger, cloves, salt, and orange zest. Pulse until combined, about 10 times. Again, use a rubber spatula to scrape the bottom of the food processor, then pulse 2 or 3 more times.

3. Remove the processor bowl from the machine, remove the blade, and use the spatula to stir the mixture until smooth. Fold in the pecans and then pour the filling into the pie crust. Smooth the top.

4. Bake until the the filling is set, 50 to 55 minutes. Remove the pie from the oven, and let it cool completely to room temperature. Then refrigerate until set so you can get a nice, clean slice when you cut it.

---

storage The pie can be made up to 1 day before serving, and it will keep for up to 3 days, covered, in the refrigerator.

---

note: The recipe was tested with a deep dish 9-inch pie dish. You can use a shallow 9-inch pie plate but you may have a little bit of filling leftover.

Me, my mom, and my niece Athena

Cooking Sweet Potatoes

There are several ways to cook sweet potatoes:

MICROWAVING is a fast and easy method. Rinse the sweet potatoes to remove any dirt, then prick them with a fork all over so steam can escape. Microwave for 5 minutes, then turn them over and microwave for an additional 5 minutes. Check for doneness: a fork should pierce the flesh with ease and little pressure. If not, continue to microwave, checking every 1 to 2 minutes (larger potatoes will take longer). With microwaving, it's possible to overcook the potatoes, so if they appear as though they are drying out, take note and cook for a shorter time next time. When the sweet potatoes are cooked through, remove them from the microwave and cut into quarters so the steam can escape. As they cool slightly, the skin will slide right off. Refrigerate until ready to use.

ROASTING IN THE OVEN is the most time-consuming method, but the results are consistent and stellar. Preheat the oven to 375°F. Rinse the sweet potatoes to remove any dirt, then prick them with a fork all over so steam can escape. Wrap them in foil, then bake on a baking sheet until a fork pierces the flesh with ease and little pressure, about 60 minutes. Remove from the oven and let cool; the skin will slide right off.

BOILING sweet potatoes has gotten a bad rap. People say the potatoes get waterlogged. But this method is so simple, and it's how my mom has always cooked her sweet potatoes for Candied Sweet Potato Pie (page 153). Here's the trick: Place the potatoes, whole, in a pot of boiling water; the water should cover the potatoes. Boil until a fork pierces the flesh easily. Then transfer the potatoes to a bowl and place in the refrigerator for a few hours; any water released will accumulate in the bottom of the bowl and won't end up in your pie.

Banoffee Pie

MAKES ONE 9-INCH PIE

Before I competed on *The Great American Baking Show*, I was a fan of *The Great British Bake Off*, though I found myself utterly confounded by the vocabulary and seemingly polite competition. This was a world where "biscuits" are cookies, bar cookies are "tray bakes," and cakes are "puddings"! Plus, unlike the fierce spirit on American cooking shows, the competition seemed downright amicable.

I recall being introduced to the portmanteau banoffee pie, a mashup of banana cream pie, dulce de leche, and banana pudding. I assumed the "offee" in its name was for *coffee*, but in true British fashion it stood for *toffee*. In my version, I add peanut butter to the whipped cream because peanut butter and bananas are so great together (and, yes, so American!). You might be wondering if toffee in a pie adds too much sweetness. I wondered the same thing, but I kept finding myself going back to the fridge for another slice!

6 tablespoons (85g) **unsalted butter**

6 tablespoons (75g) packed **light** or **dark brown sugar**

1 (14.5-ounce) can **sweetened condensed milk**

¼ teaspoon **kosher salt**

1 **Graham Cracker Pie Crust** (page 171), baked

3 ripe **bananas**

1 cup (240ml) **heavy cream**

3 tablespoons (48g) **creamy peanut butter**

2 tablespoons (15g) **confectioners' sugar**

1 teaspoon **vanilla extract**

2 ounces **dark chocolate**, finely chopped and melted

1. Combine the butter and brown sugar in a medium saucepan over medium heat. Stir occasionally, until the sugar dissolves into the butter. Whisking constantly, pour in the condensed milk and heat until it starts to boil, thicken, and take on a little color, like a blond caramel, 5 to 7 minutes. Let the mixture bubble for 2 to 3 more minutes—the bubbles will be slow at first, but then will be more frequent. Remove from the heat and stir in the salt.

2. Pour the toffee filling into the graham cracker crust and let cool at room temperature for 30 minutes, then cover and transfer to the refrigerator to chill for at least 4 hours or up to 3 days.

3. Peel and slice the bananas ½ inch thick. Arrange them on top of the filling.

4. Add the cream, peanut butter, confectioners' sugar, and vanilla to the bowl of a stand mixer fitted with the whisk attachment (or to a large bowl, if using a hand mixer). Whip the ingredients on medium-low speed until medium peaks form, about 3 minutes. Dollop the cream on top of the bananas and smooth into an even layer.

5. Use a spoon to drizzle the melted chocolate over the whipped cream. Refrigerate the pie, uncovered, until ready to serve.

storage If not serving within a few hours, refrigerate, covered, after step 2 for up to 3 days. Then proceed with the recipe when ready to serve.

storage Store, covered, in the refrigerator, for up to 4 days. This tart can also be frozen, wrapped tightly in plastic, for up to 2 months.

Chocolate Caramel Tart

MAKES ONE 9-INCH TART

This decadent tart has layers of chocolate and caramel, from the chocolate shortbread cookie-like crust to the chocolate-caramel ganache and creamy caramel smeared along the base of the tart and drizzled over the top. The key to balancing the sweetness of the caramel is to cook it until it's the color of cinnamon (darker caramel takes on a more robust, slightly bitter taste). Cooking caramel can be tricky because you need to actually spoon some out of the pot onto a white plate to determine the color. Also, it browns (and burns!) quickly, so once it starts to take on color, pay very close attention. But it's the chocolate that's the star of this tart. Let it shine by using really good chocolate. See the Resources (page 281) for suggested chocolate brands.

10 ounces **bittersweet chocolate**, melted

1½ cups **Creamy Caramel** (page 272; make caramel just prior to using so that it will be hot)

Chocolate Tart Crust (page 160), in a 9-inch pan, fully baked

3 large **eggs**, room temperature

Flaky sea salt

1. Spread 2 tablespoons (30g) of the caramel in a thin layer over the tart crust. Set aside ⅓ cup of caramel for drizzling on the finished tart.

2. Add the eggs to the bowl of a stand mixer fitted with the whisk attachment. Set the mixer on low speed and slowly beat the eggs for 2 minutes.

3. Increase the speed on the stand mixer to medium and whisk until the eggs are foamy. Then reduce the speed to low and drizzle in the hot caramel, carefully resting the pan along the lip of the bowl so that the hot caramel doesn't hit the moving whisk and splatter. When all the caramel has been drizzled in, increase the speed to medium high and whisk for 5 minutes. By now, the mixture should be smooth and will have cooled down a bit. Reduce the speed to low and drizzle in the melted chocolate until combined.

4. Immediately pour the mixture, all at once, into the tart crust. The mixture will promptly start to set, so don't attempt to smooth it out.

5. Transfer ⅓ cup (75g) of the caramel to a piping bag or a zip-top bag with a corner cut off (in order to achieve a piping consistency, you may need to microwave the creamy caramel slightly before adding it to the piping bag). Pipe lines of caramel 1 inch apart over the surface of the tart. Rotate the tart 90 degrees and drag a butter knife or offset spatula through the lines of caramel in one direction, then reverse direction for the second line. Continue across the tart to create a feathered effect. Lightly sprinkle with flaky salt (if desired).

6. Allow the tart to set at room temperature for 1 hour. When the filling has cooled to room temperature, sprinkle flaky sea salt on top, then transfer the tart to the refrigerator and allow to cool completely, at least 2 to 3 hours before serving. Slice and serve.

Chocolate Tart Crust

MAKES ONE 9-INCH TART CRUST

Some crusts are just crumbly shortbread cookies pressed into a tart pan and masquerading as a dough crust. This is one of those cookie-like tart crusts. The main difference is that it uses confectioners' sugar instead of granulated sugar, which makes the dough come together a little bit easier, especially if you are mixing by hand.

Note that this recipe is for an unbaked crust. Intended use determines whether you will want to bake the crust before filling. See page 173 for instructions on baking the crust either partially or fully before filling. In this instance, the chocolate in the ingredients can make it difficult to gauge doneness because color indicators (e.g., descriptive words like "golden brown") don't apply. By using other senses, like smell and touch, you will be able to determine when the crust is done. When ready, it should look dry, like it's just about to crack, and with light pressure it should feel dry (but it might leave a buttery residue on your fingertips).

1¼ cups (150g) **all-purpose flour**

2 tablespoons (10g) **unsweetened cocoa powder**

Dash of **kosher salt**

6 tablespoons (85g) **unsalted butter**, room temperature, cut into ½-inch pieces

½ cup (60g) **confectioners' sugar**

1 large **egg**, room temperature

1. Sift the flour and cocoa powder together into a small bowl, then whisk in the salt.

2. In the bowl of a stand mixer fitted with the paddle attachment, cream the butter and confectioners' sugar on medium-low speed until pale and fluffy, 4 to 5 minutes.

3. Add the egg to the butter mixture and continue mixing on medium-low speed until it comes together, about 2 additional minutes. If your mixture looks separated after a couple of minutes of mixing, don't worry—it will come together during the next step.

4. Reduce the mixer speed to low and add the flour mixture a heaping tablespoon at a time. Don't overwork the dough during this step. Stop the mixer just as the dough clumps together.

5. Use a rubber spatula to transfer the dough to a work surface. If there are any stubborn bits of flour that aren't incorporated, knead them into the dough. Shape the dough into a disk, wrap it in plastic, and refrigerate it for at least 1 hour and up to 3 days (it can also be frozen, wrapped tightly in plastic, for up to 2 months).

6. When you're ready to use the dough, place a 14-inch sheet of wax or parchment paper on your work surface. Set the tart dough on the paper and place another sheet on top. Use a rolling pin to roll the dough into an 11-inch circle (for a 9-inch tart pan). Remove the top sheet of paper and use the bottom sheet to flip the dough into the tart pan. Then, remove the second piece of paper and gently press the dough into the pan, working it into all the edges. Use a rolling pin to roll over the rim of the pan, which will neatly trim the edges.

7. Refrigerate or freeze the dough for at least 30 minutes (and up to 3 days in the fridge or 2 months in the freezer).

8. Use a fork to prick the bottom of the crust all over. Line the bottom with foil or parchment paper and fill with pie weights. Bake in the center of an oven preheated to 375° F for 12 to 15 minutes. Remove the pie weights and bake an additional 6 to 8 minutes, until set and dry. Remove from the oven and set on a cooling rack.

Passion Fruit Tart

MAKES ONE 9-INCH ROUND TART OR ONE 14-INCH RECTANGULAR TART

The most elegant tarts supremely showcase Gestalt psychology: the whole is greater than the sum of its parts. I can't help but give a wry smile when people learn I majored in psychology. "But what are you doing with *that* degree?" they always ask. And I can't help but think of them when I think about tarts. To me, the greatest tarts prove that components not all that difficult or particularly exciting on their own can be paired to make something inspired and gorgeous. This tart was inspired by pastry chef Miro Uskokovic.

2 teaspoons **unflavored gelatin**

2 tablespoons **hot water**

½ cup (100g) **granulated sugar**

6 large **eggs**, room temperature

1 cup (240g) **passion fruit puree**

¼ cup (60ml) **lemon juice**

2 tablespoons **unsalted butter**, cold

Easy Press-in Pie Crust (page 172), in 9-inch round tart pan fully baked and cooled

Meringue (see below)

¼ cup chopped **pistachios**

1 tablespoon **dried food-grade rose petals** (optional)

FOR THE MERINGUE:

4 large **egg whites**, room temperature

¼ teaspoon **kosher salt**

½ cup (100g) **granulated sugar**

½ teaspoon **rose extract** (optional)

1. Sprinkle the unflavored gelatin over the hot water in a small bowl and allow to dissolve for at least 5 minutes. Microwave the gelatin in 20 second intervals, stirring with a fork in between until fully dissolved and set aside.

2. Meanwhile, place a medium saucepan filled with an inch or so of water over medium-low heat and allow to gently simmer. Place the sugar and eggs in a large heatproof bowl. Add the passion fruit puree and lemon juice and whisk to combine. Place the bowl over the pot of simmering water and whisk until the filling thickens and is 165°F on an instant-read thermometer.

3. Strain the filling through a fine mesh sieve into a large bowl. Whisk in the butter until melted and smooth, then stir in the dissolved gelatin. Set the filling aside for 10 minutes to cool slightly.

4. Pour the filling into the cooled tart crust and place in the refrigerator to set for 4 hours.

5. When ready to serve, make the meringue. In the bowl of a stand mixer fitted with the whisk attachment, add the egg whites and salt and whisk on medium speed until frothy, 2 minutes or so. Reduce the speed to low, then gradually add the sugar. Continue whisking on high speed until the meringue is smooth, glossy, and stiff peaks form, 2 to 4 minutes. Whisk in the rose extract, if using.

6. Dollop the meringue on top of the passionfruit layer. Use a kitchen torch to brown the meringue all over. Sprinkle with pistachios and the dried rose petals, if using. Serve immediately.

storage If not serving immediately, hold off on adding the meringue and garnish; simply cover the filled tart with plastic wrap so it touches the passionfruit layer. Refrigerate for up to 1 day before you plan to serve it. When ready to serve, add the meringue and garnish to complete it. If I bring this to a friend's home, I am super careful during transport so the meringue stays put. And I finish it with the blowtorch in front of friends for added fiery flair!

Grandma Leona's Strawberry Delight

Prepare a double batch of the Easy Press-in Pie Crust and bake it in a 9 by 13-inch baking pan and set aside to completely cool. Double the cream cheese, heavy cream, confectioners' sugar, and vanilla in the Better Together Fruit Tart and follow the mixing instructions in step 1. Spread the cream cheese filling into the cooled crust. For the fruit topping, mix 2 cups of sliced fresh strawberries into a (21-ounce) can of strawberry pie filling and spread over the cream cheese filling. Store in the refrigerator for up to 4 days.

Better Together Fruit Tart

MAKES ONE 9-INCH TART

I created this tart, which is much like a no-bake cheesecake, during the height of the Black Lives Matter protests regarding the horrific death of George Floyd in June 2020. We took to the streets to decry Breonna Taylor's and George Floyd's lives being needlessly cut short. Despite the divisiveness in the country, the fruit in this tart reminds me that we, as a people, are truly better together. We are more interesting. We get more flavors and textures and colors. We thrive during different seasons, in different climates, in different places. Some of us can withstand criticism, and some of us are delicate and must be handled with the utmost care. Some of us are a little acidic and tart and green, like a kiwi. And some of us are sugary sweet but a little firmer, like a peach.

When different fruits come together, they create a symphony of flavors. There are overtones—notes that aren't played but can be heard when certain chords are struck. That's just like us! We don't have to be a "melting pot" where we all blend together. We can be a fruit tart! We can coexist, standing shoulder to shoulder, in all of our glorious differences. We can live in harmony and are more interesting and better because of the red cherry that's adjacent to the fuchsia raspberry. Even if one of those strawberries is underripe, you won't even notice when it's next to a juicy nectarine. When we unite, we are better together.

Use whatever fresh fruits are in season. I like to leave some of the strawberry stems intact. I'll leave some berries whole and cut large ones in half to show the inside of the fruits, which adds variety to the aesthetics. A store-bought graham cracker crust also works great with this recipe!

1 (8-ounce) package (1 cup/226g) **full-fat cream cheese**

¾ cup (180ml) **heavy cream**

½ cup (60g) **confectioners' sugar**

1 teaspoon **vanilla extract**

1 **Easy Press-in Pie Crust** (page 172), baked, or 1 **Graham Cracker Pie Crust** (page 171), baked

3 cups **assorted fresh fruits** (such as strawberries, raspberries, blueberries, sliced peaches, mango, and kiwi)

¼ cup **jelly,** such as strawberry or apricot

---

1. Place the cold cream cheese, cream, confectioners' sugar, and vanilla in the bowl of a stand mixer fitted with the paddle attachment (or in a large bowl, if using a hand mixer). Beat at high speed until stiff peaks form and the filling is smooth (initially, it may be a little lumpy, but just keep beating—you want it to really thicken up).

2. Spread the cream cheese filling evenly in the tart crust. Arrange the fruits on top.

3. Heat the jelly in a small bowl in the microwave on medium-low power until liquefied, about 30 seconds. Use a pastry brush to dab the glaze in a thin layer over the fruit. Serve immediately.

---

note If your filling isn't firm after mixing, just set it in the refrigerator before arranging the fruit on top.

---

storage The tart can be refrigerated for up to 2 days before serving.

Lemon Surprise Tart

MAKES ONE 9-INCH TART

When I was in law school, I learned that one of the keys to success is to under-promise and over-deliver. I happen to be the "dream big, talk often" type, so this is something I've naturally struggled with. The strategy paid off big in the finale of *The Great American Baking Show*, when I decided to tweak one of my recipes, at the last minute, after pulling an all-nighter of vigorous testing. The tweak was to add bits of candied ginger to the lemon curd filling for my cream puffs. As I took a bite of the mouth-puckering lemon curd and landed on the sharp, peppery bit of ginger, it was like fireworks in my mouth!

Keeping a secret on the set wasn't easy with swarms of producers and cameras, but I somehow pulled it off. When Paul Hollywood took a bite of the pastry, he threw his arms into the air and yelled out, "Wow!," completely startling me. You, too, can have people exclaiming with pleasure when they bite into this stupendously delicious and easier-than-it-looks, surprising lemon tart.

4 teaspoons **cold water**

1 teaspoon **unflavored powdered gelatin**

1 tablespoon grated **lemon zest**

¾ cup (180ml) **fresh lemon juice** (from about 4 lemons)

4 large **eggs**

¾ cup (150g) **granulated sugar**

2 tablespoons (28g) **unsalted butter**

¼ cup diced **candied ginger**

1 **Easy Press-in Pie Crust** (page 172), fully baked

Vanilla Whipped Cream (page 274), unsweetened (optional)

Honey (optional)

1. Add the cold water to a small bowl and sprinkle the gelatin over the water. Use a fork to stir until well combined.

2. To a medium saucepan, add the lemon zest, eggs, and sugar and whisk vigorously until combined. Whisk in the lemon juice. Cook over low heat, whisking constantly, until the mixture is thick and creamy, about 8 minutes. The curd is done when it coats the back of a wooden spoon, and when you drag your finger across the curd on the spoon, the streak remains visible. If you see any bits of curdled egg in the lemon curd, simply strain the curd through a sieve into a separate bowl.

3. Remove the lemon curd from the heat and stir in the butter until melted. Then, stir in the gelatin mixture until just combined (the heat will melt the gelatin). Stir in the candied ginger, then pour the filling into the crust.

4. Refrigerate the tart until it's completely set, about 4 hours or up to 2 days. Serve cold, topped with the whipped cream and a drizzle of honey, if desired.

Crawfish Hand Pies

MAKES 8 HAND PIES

Natchitoches is a small town in northern Louisiana that is home to one of the best kept secrets of Louisiana cuisine: Natchitoches meat pies. I spent summers in Natchitoches when I was in middle school taking courses like Latin and trigonometry. And as much fun as academic summer camp was (no sarcasm—it really was fun!), eating the Nachitoches meat pies at the end of our four-hour drive from Baton Rouge was the most memorable part.

In an ode to my northern Louisianan brethren and sistren, here is my take on the savory Natchitoches meat pie. I use a crawfish étouffée recipe instead of the traditional meat filling (shrimp works well, too!) and bake them for gorgeous flaky layers. If you have leftover filling, save it and serve it over rice, Louisiana-style.

4 tablespoons (55g) **unsalted butter**

1 medium **yellow** or **white onion**, finely chopped

2 **celery stalks**, thinly sliced

½ **green bell pepper**, cored, seeded, and finely chopped

2 **garlic cloves**, minced

3 tablespoons (25g) **all-purpose flour**, plus more for shaping

2 tablespoons **tomato paste**

¾ cup (180ml) **white wine**

¾ cup **water**

1 to 2 tablespoons **Louisiana hot sauce**

1 dried **bay leaf**

2 teaspoons **Creole seasoning**

½ teaspoon **kosher salt**

½ teaspoon **freshly ground black pepper**

1 pound **crawfish tail meat** or **shrimp** (if using shrimp, roughly chop)

1 large **egg**

1 disk of dough for **Flaky Pie Crust** (page 140) or **store-bought pie dough**

---

1. In a large skillet, melt the butter over medium-high heat. Add the onion, celery, and bell pepper and cook, stirring occasionally, until softened, about 10 minutes. Add the garlic to the skillet and cook, stirring, until fragrant, an additional 1 minute.

2. Sprinkle 3 tablespoons flour over the ingredients and stir. Add the tomato paste and stir until it is lightly toasted, about 2 minutes.

3. Pour in the wine and water. Cook until the liquid is reduced by half, about 2 to 3 minutes. Add the hot sauce, bay leaf, Creole seasoning, salt, and pepper. Bring to a boil and cook until the mixture starts to thicken. Add the crawfish and reduce the heat to a simmer. Cook until the crawfish is cooked through and opaque, about 10 minutes. Remove from the heat and discard the bay leaf. Let cool completely before using for the filling.

4. Line a baking sheet with parchment paper and whisk the egg in a small bowl.

5. Roll the pie crust on a floured work surface to a rectangle ¼ inch thick. Work quickly because cold dough is easier to handle and preserves the flaky layers. Use a 3-inch round

RECIPE CONTINUES

cutter to cut circles of dough as close to one another as possible. Gather the scraps, reroll, and cut out more circles. You should have about 16 rounds, which is enough for 8 hand pies.

6. Place 8 rounds of dough on the baking sheet. Mound about 2 tablespoons of étouffée in the center of each of the rounds. Try to keep the étouffée in the center and leave about ½-inch border around the edge.

7. Gently brush the whisked egg around the edge of the dough, which will act like glue to hold the 2 circles of dough together. Place the remaining 8 dough rounds on top, and press the tines of a fork around the edges to seal.

8. Place the hand pies in the freezer for 15 minutes.

9. Preheat the oven to 350°F and place a rack in the middle of the oven.

10. Brush the pies all over with the remaining egg wash. Use a small, sharp knife to cut an X in the top of each pie so steam can escape during baking. Transfer the baking sheet with the pies to the oven and bake until golden all over, about 30 minutes.

11. Remove from the oven and let cool slightly before serving warm.

Graham Cracker Pie Crust

MAKES ONE 8- OR 9-INCH PIE CRUST

This classic pie crust is an easy option because it doesn't require resting, rolling, or an extended period of chilling. It's flavorful from the spices in the graham crackers, as well as from the butter. (For the ultimate "cheat code," you could purchase a ready-made graham cracker crust at the grocery store.) See page 175 for ideas on how to use this crust and what fillings work best with it.

14 whole **graham crackers** (about 225g)

¼ cup (50g) **granulated sugar**

½ cup (1 stick/113g) **unsalted butter**, melted

1. Add the graham crackers to the bowl of a food processor and process until finely ground. Add the sugar and melted butter and pulse until the crumbs are moistened and they clump together. (You can also place the crackers in a zip-top bag and use a rolling pin or a pot to crush them before stirring in the sugar and melted butter.)

2. Place the crumbs in a 9-inch pie plate and use the bottom of a measuring cup to press the crumbs firmly into an even layer in the bottom and up the sides of the pan. If using a glass pie plate, lift it up over your head to a light and let the light refract through to see if there are places that need more crumbs. Freeze the pie crust for 15 minutes so the butter hardens.

3. Preheat the oven to 350°F and place a rack in the middle of the oven.

4. Bake the crust for 10 minutes. Remove from the oven and let cool completely before proceeding.

Easy Press-in Pie Crust

MAKES ONE 9-INCH PIE CRUST OR CRUST FOR ONE 8-INCH BAKING PAN

This easy crust is more crumbly than flaky, and it can be either par-baked or fully baked before filling. It's just as buttery and delicious as a traditional pie crust, but you don't need a rolling pin! I adapted it from the very first dessert I remember making with my mom—Grandma Leona's Strawberry Delight (page 164).

Note that this recipe gives you an unbaked crust. Intended use determines whether you will want to bake the crust before filling. See opposite page for tips on either partially or fully baking the crust before filling it. And see page 174 for ideas on how to use this crust and what fillings work best with it.

1 cup (125g) **all-purpose flour**, plus extra as needed

¼ cup (30g) **confectioners' sugar**

¼ teaspoon **kosher salt**

½ cup (1 stick/113g) **unsalted butter**, melted

1. In a medium bowl, whisk together the flour, confectioners' sugar, and salt. Use a wooden spoon to stir in the melted butter until the dough comes together. It won't be crumbly like pie dough—it will be soft and sticky.

2. Transfer the mixture to a 9-inch pie pan or an 8-inch baking pan and, using lightly floured hands, press the dough evenly into the bottom and up the sides of the pan (or just press into the bottom of a pan if using a square pan). Freeze the crust for at least 20 minutes (or up to 2 months) before baking.

3. Bake at 350°F until set, 15-20 minutes.

To Pre-bake or Not to Pre-bake

How do you know when *not* to bake the crust ahead of filling it? And when do you bake the crust halfway or even completely bake it before filling? And what exactly is "blind-baking"? Here are the answers:

No pre-bake required: Some pies don't require a fully baked or pre-baked crust before the filling is added. Line the pan with the dough, add the filling, and bake completely. As long as the filling isn't too liquidy, this method works fine. It's perfect for fruit pies, cobblers, and rustic tarts.

Par-baked: When you half-bake the crust before filling, it's called par-baking. This method is used when a filling is so liquidy that it might make the crust soggy before it's had a chance to firm up in the oven, like a sweet potato pie. The crust is baked with a "faux filling" of pie weights to give the crust a head start (and avoid the dreaded "soggy bottom!").

TO PAR-BAKE A PIE CRUST:

1. Prick the dough all over with the tines of a fork. Fit a piece of aluminum foil or parchment paper on the crust, leaving enough overhang so that you use the edges to lift it out later. (I like to use foil because I can easily cover the edges to prevent them from cooking too quickly, but parchment paper works, too.)

2. Fill the tart or pie with pie weights or dried beans so the dough holds its shape and doesn't puff up.

3. Bake on the middle rack at 350°F until the bottom of the crust is dried out, about 20 minutes. You know it's ready if, when you lift out the foil or parchment, it doesn't stick. Carefully remove the pie crust from the oven by sliding it out and holding it from the bottom, so that you don't disturb the sides or edges of the crust (best to use two oven mitts).

4. Carefully remove the parchment paper or foil and the pie weights or beans. Set the pan on a cooling rack for the crust to cool, and later fill it according to the recipe's instructions.

Blind-baked: This term refers to a fully baked crust. Like the par-baked crust, this type of crust is first baked with a "faux filling" of pie weights or dried beans until the bottom of the crust dries out. Then, the weights are removed and the crust is returned to the oven and baked until it's golden brown. Blind-baked crusts are most often paired with cooked pie fillings that don't need to be baked, like the Banoffee Pie (page 156) or Lemon Surprise Tart (page 166). (Note: Graham Cracker Pie Crust, page 171, is an exception—you don't need pie weights to blind bake it).

Which Crust for Which Pie?

With so many cobblers, pies, and tarts to pair with different kinds of crusts, the following guide will help ensure you make the perfect match!

Flaky Pie Crust (PAGE 140)

This crust is so flaky that it's flaky *on fleek*. It's what the French call *pâte brisée*, or "broken pie crust." It's the most traditional and most popular type of crust for pies.

Best for: This crust is for pies that are baked in the oven, like sweet potato, pumpkin, and even pecan pie. You can also use it for savory tarts and quiches, hand pies, and rustic tarts—cobblers, too. It's a go-to for Cake Pan Quiche Lorraine (page 88), Picnic Peach Cobbler (page 137), Double-Crust Apple Pie (page 149), Bourbon Pecan Pie (page 150), Candied Sweet Potato Pie (page 153), and Crawfish Hand Pies (page 169).

Tip: If the filling is creamy and the pie must be refrigerated, a flaky pie crust will soften and lose its best characteristic—the flakiness! So, avoid using this crust for cream pies and must-be-refrigerated pies.

Easy Press-in Pie Crust (PAGE 172)

This crust is so crumbly that it's more like a shortbread cookie. It's also known as short-crust pastry, and what the French call *pâte sucrée*, or "sweetened crust." It works beautifully when pressed into tart pans, and it can be flavored with vanilla or chocolate.

Best for: This crust is excellent paired with classic sweet tarts, like the Chocolate Caramel Tart (page 159), Better Together Fruit Tart (page 165), and Lemon Surprise Tart (page 166).

Tip: The edges of tart pans go straight up and have no overhang, making these recipes best for tart or baking pans, rather than pie plates.

Graham Cracker Pie Crust (PAGE 171)

These crusts call for already-baked graham crackers, which are pulverized into fine crumbs and then mixed with butter and sugar. It is simple to prepare, but still flavorful.

Best for: Graham cracker crusts are ideal for custard and cream pies that are refrigerated, like the Banoffee Pie (page 156). The crust also is great for baked custard-y dishes, functioning as an alternative crust for the Candied Sweet Potato Pie (page 153), Better Together Fruit Tart (page 165), and Pecan Candy Cheesecake (page 204).

Tip: Although making your own crust is satisfying, you can purchase a ready-made graham cracker crust from the store, and it will work beautifully in the recipes listed.

Store-Bought Pie Crusts

These are typically flaky-style pie crusts, unless the package clearly states otherwise. Unlike homemade pie crusts, they don't need to be chilled in the refrigerator before baking. For double-crust pies, like the apple pie on page 149 or Picnic Peach Cobbler (page 137), I prefer the crust doughs that come rolled up in a box. I remove them from the refrigerator about 5 minutes before fitting them into the pie plate so that the dough can soften a bit and be easier to unroll. These commercial crusts also work great for constructing a lattice top for a pie's top crust. You can even use a rolling pin to roll out these dough rounds to your desired size.

See page 27 for video tutorial instructions on weaving a lattice crust.

CAKES

Nothing is quite as festive as cake. I'm sharing my favorite layered cakes, pound cake, sheet cake, and even cheesecake. They are all gorgeous enough to be the star centerpiece of the table. And if your layered cake should slip from melting buttercream (which sometimes happens), fret not. You can always transform the smashed cake into delicious Cake Truffles (page 214).

The Glorious
Vanilla Bean

Vanilla for bakers is like salt for cooks. It helps accentuate the flavors of everything else, from making chocolate taste more chocolaty to bringing out the carrot flavor in a carrot cake. Vanilla flavor can be so much more expressive than what you get from the small, brown bottle of cheap extract most people store at the back of the cupboard.

I embraced whole vanilla beans when I started making vanilla macarons. I bought the beans in Paris from the famed culinary boutique G. Detou for the sole purpose of making vanilla bean ganache. These vanilla beans were large—nearly a foot long, moist, and fragrant with an aroma that perfumed their entire storage area. The shopworker informed me that the shipment had just arrived from Madagascar. I bought them in packs of ten for twenty-five euros! This was in 2011, and I didn't know how good I had it.

Now, I treat vanilla beans like baking gold, mostly because they're priced as such! These days, I bake mostly with pure vanilla extract or vanilla paste to harness vanilla's superpowers in my everyday baking. Both extract and paste are more economical than the beans, although good-quality extract or vanilla paste—which includes tiny specks of vanilla bean seeds—is still a pricey investment. If you do make an investment in vanilla beans, but they dry out and harden, you can rehydrate them by soaking in hot liquid until softened. Then, they can be easily split, opened, and their speckled seeds rescued. And don't you dare toss that scraped-out pod! Allow it to dry completely, then store in your granulated sugar to impart even more vanilla flavor.

Saucepan Chocolate Cake

MAKES ONE 9-INCH CAKE

This super-chocolaty cake is so easy to prepare and so perfect in satisfying a sweet tooth that you won't hesitate to make it—even on a busy weeknight. You won't need an electric mixer, and the frosting consists of caramel poured on top. If you don't have instant coffee granules, you can use 1 tablespoon of strong brewed coffee, or just skip the coffee altogether.

Nonstick baking spray with flour

1⅔ cups (200g) **cake flour**

1 teaspoon **baking soda**

1 cup (200g) **granulated sugar**

1 teaspoon **kosher salt**

½ cup (1 stick/113g) **unsalted butter**

2 tablespoons (30ml) **vegetable oil**

⅔ cup (65g) **unsweetened cocoa powder**

2 teaspoons **instant coffee granules**

¾ cup (180ml) **water**

1 cup (240ml) **buttermilk** (see page 51)

1 large **egg** plus 3 large **egg yolks**, room temperature (see page 190)

1 teaspoon **vanilla extract**

Creamy Caramel (page 272) or store-bought caramel

1. Preheat the oven to 350°F and place a rack in the middle of the oven. Spray a 9-inch cake pan with baking spray.

2. Sift the cake flour and baking soda into a large bowl. Add the sugar and ½ teaspoon of the salt and whisk to combine.

3. To a medium saucepan, add the butter, oil, cocoa powder, coffee granules, and the water. Cook over medium heat, whisking constantly, until the butter melts and everything comes together, about 3 minutes. Remove from the heat—it's important that the mixture doesn't get too hot and start to boil.

4. Pour the cocoa mixture into the flour mixture and stir until just combined. It will be a thick, paste-like batter, similar to box brownie mix. Touch the batter to make sure it isn't hot (warm is okay). Stir in the buttermilk and then whisk in the egg, egg yolks, and vanilla just until combined. The batter will be loose and a little liquidy. It's important that you don't overmix it.

5. Pour the batter into the prepared cake pan and bake until a cake tester or toothpick comes out clean and the center is set and slightly domed, about 30 minutes. Remove from the oven and let cool on a wire rack in the pan for 10 minutes. Remove from the pan and allow to cool completely.

6. Heat the caramel in a medium heat-safe bowl in the microwave until it's a pourable consistency, about 30 seconds. Stir in the remaining ½ teaspoon salt. Pour the caramel over the cake, allowing it to drip down the sides. Slice and serve, spooning additional caramel on each slice.

Pound Cake

MAKES 2 LOAF CAKES OR 1 BUNDT CAKE

This pound cake may be the easiest cake you'll ever bake. It bakes up just as a pound cake should—with a thick outer crust, a tight-crumbed center, and a superb buttery taste. It's important that your ingredients are at room temperature; that will help them come together more easily into a thick, velvety batter.

Nonstick baking spray with flour

1½ cups (3 sticks/339g) unsalted butter, room temperature

1 (8-ounce) package (1 cup/226g) cream cheese, room temperature

2 teaspoons vanilla extract

¼ teaspoon kosher salt

3 cups (600g) granulated sugar

6 large eggs, room temperature

3 cups (375g) cake flour or all-purpose flour

Creamy Vanilla Glaze (page 276)

1. If using loaf pans, preheat the oven to 350°F (325° if using a Bundt pan) and place a rack in the middle of the oven. Spray two 9 by 5-inch loaf pans or a 10-cup Bundt pan with baking spray and set aside.

2. In the bowl of a stand mixer fitted with the paddle attachment, beat the softened butter and cream cheese on medium-low speed until smooth, creamy, and well combined, about 1 minute. Add the vanilla and salt.

3. With the mixer running on medium-low speed, pour the sugar into the bowl in a steady stream. The batter will start to take shape. Increase the speed to medium and mix until the batter becomes pale, fluffy, and has lightened in color, 4 to 5 minutes.

4. Add the eggs, 2 at a time, mixing until they are incorporated into the batter, about 1 minute for each addition. This is the perfect time to stop the mixer and use a rubber spatula to scrape the bottom and sides of the bowl. If the batter appears broken from the addition of the final 2 eggs, don't worry—it will come together with the next step.

5. Turn the mixer off and add the flour all at once. Mix on low speed just until no streaks of flour remain. Scrape the sides and bottom of the bowl and mix in any bits of flour that were not fully incorporated. Scrape the batter into the prepared pan(s) and smooth the top with the rubber spatula or back of a spoon.

6. Bake until a cake tester inserted deep into the center of the loaves or Bundt cake comes out clean, 50 to 60 minutes for loaves and 1 hour 20 minutes for a Bundt cake. Remove the cakes from the oven and cool on a wire rack for 10 minutes. Use a small offset spatula or butter knife to loosen the cakes from the pan by running it around the loaf pans (or around the inside and outside perimeters if you baked a Bundt). Invert the cake out of the pans and allow to cool on the cooling rack until room temperature before icing with vanilla glaze, slicing, and serving.

storage Once the cake is completely cooled, store at room temperature (preferably covered in a cake dome) for up to 1 week.

Perfect Every Time Bundt Pan Release:

1. Coat the inside of the Bundt pan with either baking spray (which contains flour), or make a paste with 2 tablespoons very soft butter combined with 2 tablespoons of all-purpose flour. Use a pastry brush to brush the paste in every nook and cranny.

2. After baking, remove the baked Bundt from the oven and transfer to a cooling rack for exactly 10 minutes. Then, use a small angled spatula or butter knife to carefully loosen the outer edge and inner ring of the cake by following the curves of the pan.

3. Immediately flip the cake onto the cooling rack and let it cool completely.

By Heart Cake

My dad grew up in Prairieville, a rural town fifteen miles east of Baton Rouge. When we'd visit Granny Willie Mae there, we always knew we had crossed the township line when we drove past three towering oak trees. The air got a little crisper, and the sounds of suburban Baton Rouge faded away. During my childhood, Prairieville didn't even have a stoplight. My dad's mother owned and farmed the land, growing a plethora of produce—sugarcane, tomatoes, peppers, and squash—and they harvested bush beans in the spring and pole beans in the fall. There was no shortage of fresh fruit grown on the land, either—everything from melons and berries to figs and pears.

We entered the house in the rear, through a wire screen door that opened directly into my grandmother's kitchen. From just outside the doorway, I could peer into the kitchen and see Granny's cake stand with its glass dome. Her widely acclaimed million dollar cake (see page 187) was inside—a white layered cake with a fruity filling and fluffy cream cheese frosting. Sometimes she'd fill the cake with apple jelly, sometimes with crushed pineapple. Whatever filling she used, the cake was *money*. I always knew to immediately ask for a slice. Granny's cakes never lasted long.

When I was eleven years old, my mother wisely insisted that I visit my grandmother to learn how to make this cake. My mother explained that many family recipes get lost if the one person who knows them passes before teaching someone else the recipes. She recognized my early passion for baking and decided that I should be the one to carry on this tradition; further, I was to record it in the recipe book she had purchased for me when I was just seven (the handwritten note inside the front cover says: "To Vallery, Love Mom, 1992").

It was a particularly quiet afternoon, and I arrived at Granny's house with my recipe book and pen in hand. Unlike her progeny, Granny is not the talkative type. She's generous with love but choosy with words. The simplicity and directness of the recipe she shared with me that afternoon is as straightforward and direct as she is. I recorded the following that afternoon:

Cream butter and sugar until fluffy.

Add eggs, one at a time.

Sift dry ingredients and alternate with liquids, blending well after each addition.

Add extract.

Pour batter into 3 pans.

Bake.

Cool.

Granny's cake recipe is a 1-2-3-4 cake: 1 cup of butter, 2 cups of sugar, 3 cups of flour, and 4 eggs. I added the moniker *ABCs*: Aromatics (1 teaspoon each vanilla and almond extract), Baking powder (1 tablespoon), and Cow's juice (1 cup milk). By remembering my 1-2-3-4 ABCs, I've learned this recipe by heart (and it's incredibly helpful to have a fabulous cake recipe in my back pocket). My version on page 187 may look a little different, but the results are just as good.

Now, I'm the one who bakes this cake for Granny. And each time I make her signature cake, she beams with pride.

Granny's Million Dollar Cake

MAKES ONE 3-LAYER CAKE

Baked in the right pans, these cake layers bake up perfectly flat, making them ideal for a layered cake. (There's a reason some of us weren't allowed to talk loudly or shut doors while Grandma's cakes were in the oven!) If your layers form a dome, don't worry—you can still stack them. Or you can trim off the rounded top with a serrated knife and use the scraps to make Cake Truffles (page 214). Make sure all your ingredients are at room temperature, which will help this cake whip up beautifully.

The pineapple filling should be added when the cake is still warm. It acts as a soaking syrup and melds the pineapple filling into the cake layers. But don't frost the cake until it has cooled completely (otherwise the butter-based frosting will melt right off the cake!). Also, using both almond and vanilla extracts gives the cake a more interesting, wedding-cake-like flavor—which I love.

PINEAPPLE FILLING

1 (21-ounce) can **crushed pineapple in heavy syrup** or pineapple in its own juice

¼ cup (50g) **granulated sugar** (if using pineapple in its own juice, increase to ⅓ cup/65g)

CAKE

Nonstick baking spray with flour

3 cups (375g) **all-purpose flour**

1 tablespoon (15g) **baking powder**

1 teaspoon **kosher salt**

1 cup (2 sticks/226g) **unsalted butter,** room temperature

2 cups (400g) **granulated sugar**

4 large **eggs,** room temperature

1 teaspoon **vanilla extract**

1 teaspoon **almond extract**

1 cup (240ml) **whole milk**

CREAM CHEESE FROSTING

1 (8-ounce) package (1 cup/226g) **cream cheese,** room temperature

½ cup (1 stick/113g) **unsalted butter,** room temperature

4 cups (300g) **confectioners' sugar**

1 teaspoon **vanilla extract**

---

1. Prepare the pineapple filling: In a blender or food processor, blend the pineapple on low until the consistency of applesauce, about 30 seconds. Transfer to a small saucepan, add the sugar, and heat over low until the sugar dissolves, about 5 minutes.

2. Make the cake: Preheat the oven to 350°F and place a rack in the middle of the oven. Spray three 8-inch cake pans with baking spray.

3. In a large bowl, whisk together the flour, baking powder, and salt.

4. In the bowl of a stand mixer fitted with the paddle attachment, beat the butter on medium-low speed until creamy, about 30 seconds. With the mixer running, pour the sugar in a steady stream. Continue to beat on medium-low speed until incorporated, about 2 minutes. Increase the speed to medium and continue to beat until light, fluffy, and pale, 2 to 3 more minutes.

5. Add the eggs, one at a time, beating until each is incorporated before adding the next, about 2 minutes in total. Use a rubber spatula to scrape the sides and bottom of the bowl. Add the vanilla and almond extracts.

RECIPE CONTINUES

6. Reduce the mixer speed to low and add one-third of the flour mixture, mixing until just a few streaks of flour remain. Add half the milk and mix until combined. If the batter appears broken, don't worry—the next bit of flour will bring it back together. Add half the remaining flour mixture and continue to mix on low speed, just until no streaks of flour remain. Add the remaining ½ cup milk, continuing mixing on low, then add the remaining flour mixture. Mix until the flour is integrated, using a rubber spatula to scrape the bottom and sides of the bowl as needed. Divide the batter evenly among the prepared cake pans and smooth the top.

7. Bake until the cake layers are golden on top and a cake tester inserted in the middle comes out clean, about 25 minutes. Remove from the oven and cool on a wire rack for 15 minutes. Invert the layers onto the cooling rack to cool.

8. While the layers are on the cooling rack, spread half the pineapple filling on one layer and the remaining filling on a second layer. (The third layer won't get any pineapple on top.) Let cool completely.

9. Make the cream cheese frosting: Add the cream cheese, butter, confectioners' sugar, and vanilla to the bowl of a stand mixer fitted with the paddle attachment. Mix on low speed until the ingredients come together, then increase the speed to medium and mix until creamy, about 5 minutes.

10. Place one layer with pineapple filling on a cake plate, pineapple side up. Set the second layer with pineapple filling on top of the first. Then add the final plain layer, placing it upside down on top so that the bottom of the cake, the most even side, faces up (this gives you a nice, flat surface to frost). Use a spatula to frost the top and sides of the cake with the cream cheese frosting. Let the frosting set, then enjoy.

---

storage Store the cake, covered (I like using a cake dome), until ready to serve. If it won't be eaten within a couple of days, it can be stored in the refrigerator for up to 5 days.

Jelly Cake

Jelly cakes are a Southern tradition. When I went to Grandma Willie Mae's house, sometimes she would bless us with not one of her million dollar cakes but *two*. The first one was always filled with pineapple and the second one always had apple jelly as the filling. I later learned that "jelly cake" was actually a thing, traditionally filled *and* iced with jelly so it luxuriously drips down the sides. Granny always frosted her jelly cake with cream cheese frosting on the top and sides—she liked things tidy.

To turn Granny's Million Dollar Cake into a jelly cake, substitute 1 to 1½ cups of your favorite jelly for the pineapple and warm the jelly slightly to make it spreadable. It can be hard to find apple jelly these days, so I often use strawberry or apricot jam instead. Just be careful if you choose to use preserves, which contain large pieces of fruit that might not be so spreadable or beautiful for your jelly cake.

Prediction Lemon Chiffon Cake

MAKES ONE 9-INCH CAKE

I was warned early on in my career that it's difficult for women attorneys to be taken seriously, especially Black women attorneys. I was advised not to bring cakes and cookies to the office each week "like some sort of den mother." I adhered to this advice, which was hard because even as a young lawyer, I loved to bake. I decided to make an exception for birthdays, and I relished these opportunities to bake something special for the people I spent more daylight hours with than anyone else. For my boss's birthday, this lemon chiffon cake was the perfect choice: it's fancy without being fussy; it's just one layer, so taking it on the subway would be a breeze; and it's not the typical heavily frosted "birthday cake" that people expect.

True story: The next day, my boss Joe Baranello came to work and told me he dreamed I was competing on *The Great British Bake Off*, leading me to believe this cake must have magical, clairvoyant-giving powers, as I was in the in-between period of having auditioned for *The Great American Baking Show*. I didn't yet know the results of that audition—and I hadn't told a soul! Not long after, I was selected as a contestant. And I'm certain this cake earned me the goodwill from my boss that enabled me to miss five weeks of work during the filming, given that he had predicted the whole thing, after all!

This cake will bake up to the brim—you will definitely need a cake pan with 2-inch sides. A dusting of confectioners' sugar is all it needs, but you could add a dollop of Lemon Curd (page 278) and berries, if you want to be fancy.

Softened butter, for greasing the pan

4 large eggs, separated, room temperature

½ cup (60ml) water

⅓ cup (80ml) vegetable oil

Grated zest and juice from 1 lemon

1¼ cups (150g) all-purpose flour

1½ teaspoons baking powder

¾ cup plus 5 tablespoons (210g) granulated sugar

Confectioners' sugar

---

1. Preheat the oven to 325°F and place a rack in the middle of the oven. Lightly grease the bottom of a nonstick 9-inch cake pan with butter. (Do not grease the sides; the chiffon cake needs to grip onto the sides of the pan to climb its way up the pan.)

2. In a large bowl, whisk together the egg yolks, water, oil, lemon zest, and lemon juice until well combined, about 15 seconds. Sift in the cake flour and baking powder and add 5 tablespoons (60g) of the granulated sugar. Use a spoon and stir until combined. The mixture will resemble cornbread batter and should be thick yet smooth with no lumps.

3. In the bowl of a stand mixer fitted with the whisk attachment, whisk the egg whites on medium speed for 2 minutes. Increase the speed to high and add the remaining ¾ cup (150g) granulated sugar in a steady stream. Whisk on high speed until the meringue transforms from a thick white, gluey liquid to voluminous, airy puffs, about 5 minutes.

RECIPE CONTINUES

If you dip a spatula straight in and pull it out, the meringue should curl and make a small hook indicating stiff peaks (see Note). (Be careful not to over-whisk; you don't want the meringue to start to deflate or become overly stiff and dry.)

4. Use your biggest, sturdiest rubber spatula to dollop one-fourth of the meringue into the chiffon batter, stirring until the chiffon batter loosens.

5. Gently fold in the remaining meringue until there are no white streaks and all the batter is the same pale yellow color (don't overmix or you risk deflating the air incorporated into the meringue). Gently pour the batter into the prepared cake pan, and smooth with a rubber spatula so that the batter is evenly distributed in the pan.

6. Bake until golden on top, slightly domed, and the cake springs back if you gently press the top with your fingertips, 35 to 40 minutes. Remove from the oven, invert onto a cooling rack and let rest for 10 minutes, upside down (much like an angel food cake that's baked in a tube pan, this cake condenses as it cools; flipping it over makes it easier to remove from the pan). When cooled, flip over, run a small metal cake spatula or a butter knife around the rim of the pan, then remove the cake. Serve the cake dusted with confectioners' sugar.

Room Temperature Ingredients in Cakes

I have a habit of leaving eggs out on the counter in the morning on the day I plan to bake so that they'll be at room temp once it's time to use them. If you forget to take them out, just put whole eggs in a bowl of warm water for about 5 minutes, which will quickly bring them to room temperature. If you forget to leave the butter and cream cheese out at room temp, you can zap them in the microwave for about 15 seconds (be sure to remove any metallic wrapping first!). You don't want them to melt—they should be pliable, so if you press your finger into the middle, it leaves an indention.

storage Store, covered, for up to 3 days.

note To test for stiff peaks, turn off the mixer, stick a thin, long metal spatula or butter knife straight down, bring it straight up, and see a thin, narrow bit of glossy white meringue that bends just down like a shepherd's crook, as if making a smile.

VARIATION

Orange Chiffon

Substitute the grated zest of 1 orange and 1 tablespoon fresh orange juice for the lemon zest and juice.

Boosting Flavor
for a Bargain

Vanilla may be baking gold (see page 179), but there are other amazing extracts and liqueurs that can also boost the flavor in your baking recipes. Flavored liqueurs are a less pricey substitute for extracts. You may not get the exact flavor profile from almond liqueur as you would from almond extract, but that makes for even more exciting baking. A good rule of thumb is to substitute double the amount of liqueur for the amount of extract called for in the recipe. I like to stick to the same flavor base, but if you use a different flavor base just make sure the flavors complement the other ingredients in the recipe. The following are some useful flavor substitutions:

ALMOND EXTRACT ⟶ almond liqueur, such as Amaretto

VANILLA EXTRACT ⟶ rum, brandy

   IN CHOCOLATE RECIPES: chocolate liqueur, such as Godiva Dark Chocolate or Patron XO Dark Cocoa

   IN FRUIT RECIPES: cherry liqueur or kirsch liqueur

   IF ORANGE IS IN THE RECIPE: orange liqueur, such as Cointreau or Grand Marnier

   IF NUTS ARE FEATURED: any nut-based liqueur, such as Amaretto, or a hazelnut liqueur, like Frangelico

ORANGE EXTRACT ⟶ add an extra teaspoon grated orange zest, plus orange liqueur, such as Cointreau, Grand Marnier, or Patrón Citrónge

PEPPERMINT EXTRACT ⟶ peppermint liqueur, like Peppermint Schnapps

LEMON EXTRACT ⟶ add an extra teaspoon lemon zest, plus lemon liqueur, such as Limoncello

INSTANT COFFEE POWDER ⟶ coffee liqueur, such as Kahlúa or Bailey's Espresso Crème

Almost-Ate-the-Plate Carrot Cake

MAKES ONE (8-INCH) 3-LAYER CAKE OR ONE (9-INCH) 2-LAYER CAKE

My dad loves this cake so much that when he divorced his first wife, he took this recipe along with him. I've been making this cake for my dad's birthday since I was twelve years old. It's chock-full of the good stuff: fresh carrots, toasted pecans, shredded coconut—even juicy pineapple. The layers are sandwiched with a delectable cream cheese frosting.

Flavor and deliciousness aside, the best part about this cake is that it's a mix-and-bake—a one-bowl cake. In this rare bit of baker's luck, the effort required is inversely proportional to the taste: easy to make yet tastes so darn good. The recipe calls for vegetable oil, so you don't even have to break out the mixer to cream the butter and sugar. I once received the ultimate compliment from a colleague after bringing her a piece of this cake; she returned the empty plate with a Post-it note, scribbled in wide permanent marker: "I almost ate the plate."

Nonstick baking spray with flour

4 medium carrots

3 large eggs

¾ cup (180ml) vegetable oil

¾ cup (180ml) buttermilk (see page 51)

2 teaspoons vanilla extract

2 cups (400g) granulated sugar

½ teaspoon kosher salt

2 cups (250g) all-purpose flour

2 teaspoons baking soda

2 teaspoons ground cinnamon

1 (8-ounce) can crushed pineapple, drained

3½ ounces (about 1½ cups) sweetened or unsweetened shredded coconut

1 cup (120g) pecans, toasted and roughly chopped

1 recipe cream cheese frosting (see page 187)

1. Preheat the oven to 350°F and place a rack in the middle of the oven. Spray three 8-inch cake pans with baking spray. (Alternatively, use two 9-inch cake pans.)

2. Shred the carrots in a food processor or with a box grater. You will need 2 packed cups of shredded carrots.

3. In a large bowl, whisk together the eggs and vegetable oil. Add the buttermilk, vanilla, sugar, and salt and whisk until smooth.

4. Sift in the flour, baking soda, and cinnamon and use a wooden spoon to stir until no streaks of flour remain. Add the carrots, pineapple,

RECIPE CONTINUES

coconut, and pecans. Stir until the ingredients are evenly dispersed throughout.

5. Divide the batter evenly among the prepared pans and use the back of a spoon to smooth the tops. Bake until a toothpick inserted into the center comes out clean, 35 to 40 minutes.

6. Place the cake layers, still in the pans, on a wire rack. Let the cake layers cool in the pans for 15 minutes, then invert to remove. Return the cake layers to the rack to cool completely.

7. Place one cake layer on a serving tray or cake plate. Dollop some frosting on top and smear it evenly using a spatula, starting in the center of the layer and working your way to the edge. Place the second layer on top and dollop more frosting on top, spreading it evenly. Add the final layer and spread some frosting on top. Then frost the sides, using an offset spatula or pastry scraper to achieve a smooth effect. Serve.

note This recipe also works well to make a single-layer 9 by 13-inch cake.

Wartime, the Liberation of Black Women, and Cake Mix

I rarely use boxed cake mix these days, but I'm not knocking it. Cake mix may have liberated women from home kitchens as much as World War II.

Despite the differences in my grandmothers' upbringings—one was accustomed to city life and a high school graduate, while the other came from a family of prolific farmers—their lives were in some ways mirror images. They both married respected men and had families of their own. And they both worked for white

The Johnson family at my grandfather's job during "Family Day" at the Chrysler plant in Indianapolis, 1953. (My grandparents and uncle—Leona, David Jr., and Sr.)

families as "domestics"—toiling during the day cleaning and cooking and taking care of other people's children before going home to take care of their own children and their own homes. My Southern grandma, Willie Mae, did this for the meager sum of $4 a day (a fraction of what her husband, LC, earned at the time doing various jobs, $12 a day). Nine hundred miles to the north, my maternal grandmother did the same. Until World War II.

The war may have liberated white women from their own homes, but it liberated Black women from white women's homes. Grandma Leona was able to get a job at Real Silk, a manufacturing company in Indianapolis. To assist in the war effort, the company shifted its production from lady's stockings to parachutes. White women sewed silk parachutes for the soldiers, while Black women (including my grandmother) were relegated to sewing cotton parachutes for supply drops. Nevertheless, Grandma Leona never worked as a "domestic" again, and eventually climbed the ranks as a civil servant working for the federal government.

But a working mom is still a working mom. Grandma Leona's baking was limited to birthday cakes for nephews and cobblers for church picnics, as she was also putting dinner on the table for her husband and three children each night. She unapologetically used cake mixes to make celebratory cakes, like her Punch Bowl Cake (page 198). There is no shame in using cake mixes.

Punch Bowl Cake

SERVES 18

Grandma Leona made this cake with just about all the ready-made ingredients you can think of, like box cake mix, Jell-O pudding, jarred maraschino cherries, and Cool Whip. This cake wasn't just delicious, it was my *favorite*. The lightness and fruitiness were perfect for summertime, and since I'm a July baby, I always requested it for my birthday cake. My grandmother and mother always made it in the same small punch bowl they'd use for serving a half 7UP, half juice concoction for Easter brunch.

Punch bowls feel like part of a bygone era, and I've used everything from a clear glass bowl to a trifle dish for this cake.

---

1 box **yellow cake mix**, prepared and baked according to directions

2 (5.1-ounce/144g each) boxes **instant vanilla pudding**, prepared according to directions

1 (20-ounce/567g) can **crushed pineapple**

1 (21-ounce/595g) can **cherry** or **strawberry pie filling**

1 (16-ounce/454g) container whipped topping, such as **Cool Whip** or 2 batches (4 cups total) **Vanilla Whipped Cream** (page 274)

½ cup (2-ounce/60g) **chopped pecans**, toasted

1 (6-ounce/170g) jar **maraschino cherries**

---

storage This cake is refreshing during hot, summer months and should be stored in the refrigerator for up to 2 days.

1. Remove the cake from the pan and place on a cutting board. Cut the cake into 1-inch cubes.

2. Layer half the cake cubes in the bottom of a punch bowl or trifle dish. Dollop half the vanilla pudding on top. Spoon half the crushed pineapple (with juice) on top of the pudding in an even layer, followed by half the pie filling and finally, half the whipped topping. Repeat this step with the remaining cake, pudding, crushed pineapple, and pie filling.

3. Decorate the top with the remaining whipped topping, chopped pecans, and maraschino cherries.

4. Store in the refrigerator to chill. To serve, use a large spoon or serving utensil, and dip straight down to scoop out into a bowl.

Blackberry Lemon King Cake

MAKES ONE GIANT CAKE

King cake is my favorite part of Louisiana's Carnival season. This cake is eaten in the months leading up to Mardi Gras, and a plastic baby is always hidden inside. Whoever gets the piece with the plastic baby has to bring the next king cake! The traditional filling is cinnamon, but I created this version for *The Great American Baking Show* because the bright berry filling and lemony tang perfectly balance the sugary sweet glaze. This cake won me "Star Baker" for bread week, and after one bite, you'll see why!

2½ cup **fresh blackberries**

½ cup (100g) **granulated sugar**

Zest and juice from 1 **lemon**

Dough for Challah (page 231), prepared through step 6

1 large **egg**

Creamy Vanilla Glaze (page 276)

¼ cup each **purple, green,** and **yellow sugar** (see Note)

note Make your own colored sugar by massaging a few drops of food coloring into ¼ cup (50g) of granulated sugar until you get the desired color. The more food coloring you use, the deeper the color you will achieve. To take things up a notch and add flavor to the sugar, add zest from 2 lemons to the yellow sugar after it's reached the desired color, and use your fingertips to massage it in. To the purple sugar, add 1 tablespoon of freeze-dried blackberries that have been pulverized in a spice grinder to the finest texture you can achieve, then sifted. (You can discard the blackberry seeds that don't make it through the sifter.) You can also flavor other colored sugars: add orange zest to orange sugar, pulverized freeze-dried strawberries to pink sugar, and pulverized freeze-dried raspberries to red sugar.

1. Prepare the blackberry filling: Combine the blackberries, sugar, lemon zest, and lemon juice in a small or medium saucepan. Smash the blackberries and stir. Heat over medium, stirring occasionally, until thickened, about 10 minutes. Remove from the heat, transfer to a separate bowl, and allow to cool completely before using.

2. Line a baking sheet with parchment paper.

3. Divide the challah dough into 2 equal pieces and roll each piece into a rope that's 18 inches long. Roll the ropes to rectangles that are 6 to 8 inches wide.

4. Smear blackberry filling on the rectangles, leaving a 1-inch border on all sides, then roll tightly like a jelly roll.

5. Twist the 2 rolls, then bring the ends together to form an oval ring on the prepared baking sheet.

6. Cover with a clean dish towel until risen and doubled in size, about 45 minutes. Preheat the oven to 350°F.

7. Beat the egg in a small bowl. Brush egg wash all over the loaf.

8. Transfer the loaf to the oven and bake until browned, 30 to 35 minutes.

9. Remove from the oven and transfer to a cooling rack to cool completely.

10. Cover with vanilla glaze and sprinkle with purple, green, and yellow sugar before serving.

Pecan Candy Cheesecake

MAKES ONE 8-INCH CHEESECAKE

Whenever I make this cheesecake for a party, my winning dessert from *The Great American Baking Show* finale, it's always the first thing to disappear. The buttery, brown sugary pecan crust is reminiscent of pecan candy, an ode to Louisiana, while the dreamily creamy, slightly tangy filling is a lemony-rich homage to New York's signature dessert, the cheesecake. Sometimes, just to show off, I add even more layers of texture and tartness by topping it with freshly whipped cream and berries, see cheesecake photo on page 176, or drizzling warm, creamy caramel directly over the cheesecake to contrast the chilled interior.

The cheesecake gets its sublime texture because it's baked in a water bath—kind of like a mini Jacuzzi. The water bath ensures the cheesecake is baked gently, while providing a steamy environment that makes for an extra creamy cheesecake. Plus, the water bath encourages the cheesecake's top to remain perfectly flat, a geometric feat in a world of cracked top cheesecakes.

PECAN CANDY CRUST

⅓ cup **pecans**, roughly chopped

¾ cup (90g) **all-purpose flour**

½ teaspoon **baking powder**

¼ teaspoon **kosher salt**

½ cup (100g) packed **light** or **dark brown sugar**

6 tablespoons (85g) **unsalted butter**, melted

CHEESECAKE FILLING

2 (8-ounce) packages **cream cheese**, room temperature

1 cup (200g) **granulated sugar**

3 large **eggs**, at room temperature

⅓ cup (80ml) **heavy cream**, room temperature

⅓ cup (80ml) **sour cream**, room temperature

1 tablespoon **vanilla extract**

Zest of 1 **lemon**

Juice of ¼ **lemon**

Vanilla Whipped Cream, for serving (page 274; optional)

Berries, caramel, or **toasted pecans,** for serving (optional)

1. Preheat the oven to 350°F. Cut two 14-inch strips of parchment paper, and place a rack in the center of the oven. Place one strip in an 8 by 8-inch baking pan so the ends hang over the edges (they'll help you lift the cheesecake from the pan). Place the second strip perpendicular to the first, letting the ends hang over the edges.

2. Make the pecan candy crust: Add the pecans to a sheet pan and bake until toasted and fragrant, about 7 minutes. Remove the pecans from the oven and set aside. Keep the oven on.

3. Meanwhile, add the flour, baking powder, and salt to a large bowl and whisk to combine. Add the brown sugar and melted butter and stir until combined. Lastly, stir in the toasted pecan pieces. Use the bottom of a measuring cup (or your hands!) to press the mixture into the bottom of the pan in an even layer. (Don't press the crust up the sides of the pan.)

4. Transfer to the oven and bake the crust until the edges dry out, the center of the crust feels firm to light pressure but still gives a little, and the bottom feels dry but buttery, about

15 to 20 minutes. Remove the pan from the oven, and reduce the temperature to 325°F.

5. Make the cheesecake filling. Fill a medium pot or teakettle with water and bring it to a boil; reduce the heat to low and cover the pot to keep the water hot (this water bath is for baking the cheesecake).

6. In the bowl of a stand mixer fitted with the paddle attachment, beat the cream cheese on medium-high speed until it's smooth and creamy, about 2 minutes. Reduce the speed to medium-low and sprinkle in the sugar in a steady stream. Increase the speed to medium and beat until combined, about 1 minute. Increase the speed to medium-high and beat until the mixture is light and fluffy, about 1 additional minute. Use a rubber spatula to scrape down the bottom and sides of the mixing bowl as needed.

7. Reduce the speed to low and add the eggs, one at a time, making sure each is incorporated before adding the next and scraping down the sides and bottom of the bowl as needed between additions. Add the heavy cream, sour cream, vanilla, lemon zest, and lemon juice. Mix on medium until the mixture is smooth, about 2 minutes.

8. Pour the filling into the cooled crust.

9. Pull the middle oven rack halfway out and place an empty 9 by 13-inch baking pan or roasting pan in the oven. Place the cheesecake inside of the larger baking pan. Carefully pour the hot water into the large baking pan, taking care not to splash into the square pan with the cheesecake. Add enough water so that it rises halfway up the sides of the smaller pan.

10. Bake the cheesecake until it jiggles only slightly when the pan is shaken, and if you gently touch it, your finger doesn't leave an impression, about 50 to 60 minutes.

11. Carefully remove the large pan from the oven, taking care not to spill the hot water. Allow the cheesecake to cool in the hot water bath for 30 minutes. Then, remove it from the water bath and allow it to cool at room temperature for 30 minutes.

12. Transfer the cheesecake to the refrigerator for at least 4 hours before serving. Once completely chilled, carefully remove it from the square pan by lifting the parchment paper out of the pan and placing it onto a platter. Refrigerate, covered, and finish with berries, caramel, or toasted pecans before serving, if using.

---

notes It is important that all of the ingredients are at room temperature so that they will combine easily. Also, be sure to use full-fat cream cheese that is in a block (not the whipped stuff). "Whipped" cream cheese contains additives to make it fluffy—and those additives don't like to be heated and will make your cheesecake grainy.

---

make ahead This cheesecake can be prepared in advance and stored in the refrigerator for up to 3 days. The pecan candy crust can also be made up to 3 days in advance. This cheesecake freezes beautifully—just wrap tightly and allow to defrost in the refrigerator before serving.

Sheet Cake It!

Sheet cakes don't get enough love. They're easy to assemble, frost, and transport. To convert a recipe for a layered cake into a sheet cake, reduce the oven temperature by 25°F and increase the bake time. You know the sheet cake is done when a toothpick inserted into the center comes out clean.

Red Velvet Sheet Cake

MAKES ONE 9 BY 13-INCH CAKE

Cakes made with vegetable oil are always extra moist, and this oil-based red velvet sheet cake is no exception. Despite this cake's Southern roots, I became enamored of it when I lived in Los Angeles and I'd treat myself to a square of the sheet cake from The Cobbler Lady, a bakery in the Leimert Park neighborhood, on Crenshaw Boulevard. The bakery may no longer be around, but I ended up adapting this recipe (which has a hint of chocolate flavor from cocoa powder) from one of the first baking books to earn a spot on my cookbook shelf in Los Angeles—*Martha Stewart's Cupcakes*—and it's perfect paired with Granny Willie Mae's classic cream cheese frosting.

Nonstick baking spray with flour

2½ cups (300g) **cake flour**

3 tablespoons (24g) **unsweetened cocoa powder**

1 teaspoon **kosher salt**

1½ cups (360ml) **vegetable oil**

1½ cups (300g) **granulated sugar**

2 large **eggs**, room temperature

2 teaspoons **vanilla extract**

1 teaspoon **liquid red food coloring**

1 cup (240ml) **buttermilk** (see page 51)

1 teaspoon **baking soda**

1½ teaspoons **distilled white vinegar**

½ recipe **cream cheese frosting** (see page 187)

storage Store, covered, for up to 4 days.

1. Preheat the oven to 350°F and place a rack in the middle of the oven. Spray a 9 by 13-inch baking pan with baking spray.

2. Sift the cake flour, cocoa, and salt into a large bowl. In the bowl of a stand mixer fitted with the paddle attachment, beat the oil and sugar on medium-high speed until combined, about 20 seconds. Reduce the speed to medium and add the eggs, one at a time, beating until each is incorporated before adding the next, 1 minute total. Add the vanilla and red food coloring and mix until combined.

3. Reduce the mixer speed to low and add about one-third of the flour mixture. Take care not to overmix during this step. Add half the buttermilk and mix until combined. Add half the remaining flour mixture and continue to mix on low speed, just until no streaks of flour remain. Add the remaining ½ cup buttermilk, continuing to mix on low speed. Then add the remaining flour mixture. Scrape the sides and bottom of the bowl. The batter will be very loose and almost liquidy.

4. Combine the baking soda and vinegar in a small bowl. Pour it into the cake batter and mix on medium speed until just combined, about 10 seconds. Immediately pour the cake batter into the prepared pan.

5. Bake until the cake is set and a cake tester inserted in the middle comes out clean, 25 to 30 minutes. Remove the cake from the oven and set on a wire rack until completely cooled, about 30 minutes.

6. Spread the frosting on top of the cake. Cut and serve.

Pecan Bundt Cake

MAKES 1 BUNDT CAKE

Whenever I'm home in Louisiana, the first conversation I have with my dad can be summed up with the same one-line Mad Libs story: "Vallery, make a [insert dessert here]." Most recently, it was "Vallery, make me a pecan cake." Since I'm somewhere between a dutiful daughter and a recovering people pleaser, I always oblige. It doesn't quite matter if I've tasted (or even heard of) the dessert requested.

My research often starts (and usually ends) in one of the browning pages of a recipe book that's shelved in my mom's closet. I found a weathered page offering a gem of a recipe for pecan cake. The lawyer in me proceeded with negotiations: "Dad, I'll make you this pecan cake if you bring me five pounds of pecans." I didn't need to mention that I wanted *Louisiana* pecans—those are the only kind my dad knows. Dad brought back pecans aplenty, enough for the cake and extra for me to take home to New York. This cake has a tight crumb, like a pound cake, but it's moist and full of flavor from the pineapple and nuts.

Nonstick baking spray with flour

3 cups (375g) **all-purpose flour**

1 teaspoon **baking powder**

1 teaspoon **kosher salt**

1½ cups (3 sticks/339g) **unsalted butter**, room temperature

1½ cups (300g) packed **light** or **dark brown sugar**

4 large **eggs**

1 teaspoon **vanilla extract**

2 cups (240g) roughly chopped **pecan pieces**, toasted

¾ cup (180g) canned **crushed pineapple**, in its own juice

½ cup **golden raisins**

1. Preheat the oven to 325°F and place a rack in the middle of the oven. Spray a 12-cup Bundt pan with baking spray.

2. In a large bowl, combine the flour, baking powder, and salt. Whisk to combine.

3. In the bowl of a stand mixer fitted with the paddle attachment, beat the softened butter and brown sugar on medium speed until light and fluffy, about 4 minutes.

4. Add the eggs, one at a time, beating until each is incorporated before adding the next, about 2 minutes total. Add the vanilla.

5. Reduce the speed to low and add the flour mixture. Mix until just combined. Use a rubber spatula to scrape the bottom and sides of the bowl as needed.

6. Stir in the pecans, pineapple, and raisins. Pour into the prepared pan and bake until a cake tester inserted deep into the cake comes out completely clean, 1 hour to 1 hour 15 minutes.

7. Let the cake cool in the pan on a cooling rack for 10 minutes. Invert the pan to release the cake and allow the cake to cool completely before slicing and serving.

storage This cake can be stored, covered, at room temperature for up to 1 week.

Christmas
in September

I'm always asked what the winning dish was on *The Great American Baking Show*—the one dessert that won me my title. Well, it all happened on a balmy September night in England. Snowflakes blasted from the corners of the gardens at Pinewood Studios. Gospel singers clad in choir robes sang hearty renditions of "Deck the Halls!" and "Joy to the World." Despite the warm evening, I was bundled up in a knee-length wool coat with a gray knit scarf around my neck. We were all wrapped up, brimming with holiday cheer and ready for the artificial snowstorm that deluged the outdoor set.

"Vallery, please bring your tower of treats up to the judges," Ayesha Curry, one of the hosts, directed. I picked up the three-foot-high tower that contained my slices of Pecan Candy Cheesecake (page 204), eggnog mille-feuilles, and choux rings filled with lemon cream. The sweet aroma of tangy lemon and toasted pecans wafted through the air as I inched forward from my workstation to where the judges were. The tower was heavy and blocked my vision; I struggled to keep my balance. As it swayed from side to side, Spice Adams, the other host, hopped up from his corner, offering assistance. Dropping the tower would have been a disaster and too much for my baked-out heart to handle. But I had poured my soul into these creations—this was my load to bear. I needed to take this walk alone.

I sat my tower of treats down in front of the judges, as if making a final offering at the feet of gods. And this was my judgment day. Paul Hollywood cut into the mille-feuille's inverted puff pastry, and the layers shattered with the lamination of a well-made croissant. He lifted the fork to his mouth, and with one bite, he proclaimed that I nailed both the flavor and texture of the eggnog pastry cream filling. The cheesecake was next.

Here's the thing about cheesecake: it's a squarely American dessert, yet British people *love* it. For them, it's more exotic than the daintiest French pastry. Before trying it, Paul Hollywood told a story of how he ate *eleven pieces of cheesecake* during a visit to New York City. Eleven! There was a lot riding on this cheesecake. Baking it in the water bath paid off—it was creamy and smooth. The lemon zest in the filling added a hint of brightness, and the toasty pecan candy crust added a crunchy contrast to the velvety filling. Paul Hollywood ate the entire piece and declared he'd have another. I was 2 for 2, and there was one dessert left: the choux rings with lemon cream spiked with a secret ingredient I had managed to hide from the judges earlier, when they did their rounds. There were tiny bits of candied ginger that added just enough pizzazz that Paul Hollywood shouted when he bit into it and sharply raised his arm in victory. *"That's* what I'm talking about!"

The night I won *The Great American Baking Show*, September 2017

The satisfaction of giving something every fiber of my being and having it validated is a rare feeling. And that validation is what fueled me afterward, during the many uncertainties and times of doubt that were to come. But in that moment, I knew that my best was enough. *I* was enough.

As the judges left to deliberate, we three finalists carried our towers outside, wading through the artificial snow that had by then melted into a gray mess. I carried my tower with confidence—there were no stumbles this time. My mother and sister made the trip to London with less than two days' notice, and I spotted them right in front, beaming, among the other contestants, friends, and family members.

Ayesha announced, "And the winner of *The Great American Baking Show* is . . . VALLERY!"

This was one of those surreal, out-of-body experiences I might have thought I dreamed up if there weren't actual proof. Like photos and videos proof. I was handed a crystal serving dish. This was the sole prize for winning—no cash or investment in a bakery. I hoisted the dish up into the air the way they do in sports after winning a championship and are handed the MVP trophy. My mom, sister, the other finalists, Molly and Cindy, and many of the producers and other contestants who had become friends circled around me. It was a better feeling than any Christmas morning. I did it. I *won!*

Cranberry Orange Torte

MAKES ONE 9-INCH TORTE

Brushing a glaze of simple syrup on cakes helps keep them moist while adding flavor, which is particularly helpful for layered cakes. For added pizzazz, you can decorate this torte with candied orange slices or sugared cranberries. This was the first cake I made on *The Great American Baking Show*, and you'll see why Paul Hollywood said it "tastes *divine*."

ORANGE GLAZE

¼ cup (50g) **granulated sugar**

¼ cup (60ml) **orange juice**

CRANBERRY FILLING

1 cup (120g) **fresh or frozen cranberries**

½ cup (100g) **granulated sugar**

2 tablespoons (30ml) **fresh lemon juice**

CAKE

Prediction Lemon Chiffon Cake (page 189), using orange zest instead of lemon zest; baked, removed from the pan, and cooled

½ recipe **cream cheese frosting** (see page 187), made just prior to use

make ahead The glaze and filling can be made up to 3 days in advance.

1. Make the orange glaze: Combine the sugar and orange juice in a small saucepan over medium heat. Bring to a boil, stirring until the sugar dissolves. Remove the saucepan from the heat and let cool.

2. Make the cranberry filling: Add the cranberries, sugar, and lemon juice to a medium saucepan and bring to a boil over medium-high heat. Boil, stirring often, until the cranberries begin to pop, about 5 minutes. Transfer the cranberries to a medium bowl and allow to cool, then cover and chill in the refrigerator until ready to use.

3. Assemble the cake: Use a serrated knife to cut the single layer of chiffon cake into 2 layers. Place the bottom layer on a cake board or platter, cut side up, and set the top layer aside.

4. Brush half the glaze on top of the cake layer. Spread the filling in an even layer over the cake layer.

5. Transfer the frosting to a piping bag with a large tip or use a large zip-top bag with the corner snipped off. Pipe half the frosting in an even layer on top of the cranberry filling.

6. Carefully place the other cake layer on top of the piped frosting. Brush the top layer with the remaining glaze. Dollop the remainder of the cream cheese frosting on top. Refrigerate the cake until ready to slice and serve.

Bake Your Own Adventure:
Cake Truffles

MAKES ABOUT 15 TRUFFLES

With cake and frosting or other "glue" (such as Lemon Curd, page 278), the possibilities for cake truffles are endless. Finish by dunking them in melted chocolate or candy coating for the ultimate cake truffle treat. Here's a typical formula for winning cake truffles. This also works with box cake mixes or any kind of leftover cake.

---

1 **sheet cake**

1 cup **frosting of choice**, or ⅔ cup (160ml) **milk**

1 pound finely chopped **chocolate** or **candy coating** (see Note)

3 tablespoons (45ml) **neutral oil** (like vegetable oil or melted coconut oil)

1 cup (120g) **cookie** or **graham cracker** (or more cake) **crumbs**

Additional **melted chocolate** for drizzling (optional)

---

note Candy coating makes for easier dipping than melted chocolate.

---

storage Cake truffles can be stored in an airtight container at room temperature for up to 3 days or frozen for up to 2 months. To defrost, set them out at room temperature for 3 to 4 hours.

1. Crumble the cake into a large bowl. Use your hands to make sure you get every bit of it to crumble.

2. Add the frosting or milk and use a large spoon to stir together until all of the crumbs are moistened.

3. Use your hands to roll the cake mixture and make 1½-inch-size balls. The balls should hold together easily when squished but shouldn't be too wet. If the balls don't hold together well, add a little more frosting or liquid, a tablespoon at a time.

4. Set the cake balls on a baking sheet lined with parchment or wax paper and place in the freezer while melting the chocolate.

5. Melt the chocolate in the microwave in 30-second intervals and mix in the oil. Use 2 forks to dip each cake truffle into the melted chocolate.

6. Toss the chocolate-covered truffles in the cookie crumbs to coat, coating and dipping a few at a time, then place back on the baking sheet.

7. Allow the truffles to set in the refrigerator for at least 20 minutes before serving. You may drizzle with additional melted chocolate for added flair.

RECIPE CONTINUES

Chocolate Caramel Pretzel Cake Truffles

MAKES ABOUT 12 TRUFFLES

Saucepan Chocolate Cake (page 181)

½ cup (120g) Creamy Caramel (page 272)

⅓ cup (80ml) milk

16 ounces (454g) chocolate candy coating or milk or dark chocolate

3 tablespoons (45ml) neutral oil, such as coconut oil, melted shortening, or vegetable oil

1 cup (120g) pretzel crumbs (pretzels pulverized in a food processor until fine like sand)

Million Dollar Cake Truffles

MAKES ABOUT 20 TRUFFLES

Granny's Million Dollar Cake (page 187)

1 cup (226g) cream cheese frosting (page 187)

8 ounces (227g) crushed pineapple

2 pounds (908g) white candy coating or white chocolate

6 tablespoons (90ml) neutral oil, such as coconut oil, melted shortening, or vegetable oil

Puckery Lemon Cake Truffles

MAKES ABOUT 16 TRUFFLES

Prediction Lemon Chiffon Cake (page 189)

½ cup (120g) Lemon Curd (page 278)

16 ounces (454g) white candy coating or white chocolate

3 tablespoons (45ml) neutral oil, such as coconut oil, melted shortening, or vegetable oil

1 cup (120g) cookie crumbs (cookies pulverized in a food processor until fine like sand)

Pumpkin, Ginger, and Cream Cheese Cake Truffles

MAKES ABOUT 24 TRUFFLES

Pumpkin Bread (page 52)

1 cup (226g) cream cheese frosting (see page 187), at room temperature

16 ounces (454g) white candy coating or white chocolate

3 tablespoons (45ml) neutral oil, such as coconut oil, melted shortening, or vegetable oil

½ cup (60g) store-bought gingersnap cookie crumbs (pulverize enough cookies in the food processor to yield ½ cup—they should be like fine sand)

Red Velvet Cake Truffles

MAKES ABOUT 20 TRUFFLES

Red Velvet Sheet Cake (page 207)

1½ cups (340g) cream cheese frosting (see page 187)

16 ounces (454g) white or red candy coating or white chocolate

3 tablespoons (45ml) neutral oil, such as coconut oil, melted shortening, or vegetable oil

Gathering
the Crumbs

Cake truffles are the perfect metaphor for making the most out of messy, sticky, frosting-laden circumstances. Sometimes things don't end up in the meticulous three-layer, perfectly frosted cake that you planned. Even though you buttered and floured the cake pans . . . even though you creamed the butter and sugar until it was light and fluffy . . . even when the cake was all assembled and looked *perfect* in your kitchen. Even *then*.

There was that one time when, while waiting for my train on the hot subway platform, the all-butter buttercream softened and the top two layers of my carrot cake slid right off of the bottom layer and crashed into the side of the cake box. Another time, my mom made Granny's Million Dollar Cake (page 187), then got on the plane to bring it to my sister's baby shower, *two thousand miles away in Boston*. (Yes, it got smushed while it was under the airplane seat during takeoff.)

Just because a cake (or *life!*) may not look perfect in the state it's currently in doesn't mean it can't *become* perfect with a little manipulation and creativity. Cake truffles are nothing more than cake mixed with frosting and rolled into balls. There's something homey and cute about the little balls, and I bet a lot of folks think they're even *better* than a slice of a perfect three-layered cake. In fact, they're so good that you don't have to wait for some cake catastrophe or leftover half of a cake in order to smoosh up some cake to make them. But if a cake-tastrophe does strike, take comfort in knowing your salvation is a mere truffle away.

How to
Win a Reality Show

Step 1: Get Cast

Passing the first-round interview, which is often a phone call, is easier than you may think. What's more important than what you say is how you say it: tell good stories and go off on a tangent! Casting directors want to make sure that whoever they cast likes to *talk*. Actually wanting to be on camera—or at least being unafraid of the camera—doesn't hurt, either. However, you still need whatever "special sauce" makes that show unique. For most cooking-competition shows, you need some real chops in the kitchen. The goal is to awe and inspire, so home cooks can marvel at what's possible.

Step 2: Make Friends

"I'm not here to make friends!" It's always the unlucky person who is portrayed as the villain of the show who says this. The reason this is so meaningful is that during production of a reality show, a participant is so detached from typical life that the human thing to do *is* to build relationships with others. (I spent five weeks living in a foreign country, without being able to regularly communicate with my family or friends!) It's tricky, though, because your new friends are also your competitors (something law school definitely prepared me for!). But without friends, you'll have no one to taste your two barely different chocolate shortbread cookies or teach you how to cook caramel so it doesn't burn. Without friends for support, you'll go crazy. And you'll probably go home.

The Great American Baking Show season 4 semifinalists:
Molly, Cindy, Antoinette, me, and Bryan

Step 3: Get in the Zone

You need tunnel vision. Sleep? That's a luxury. A square meal? Eating
is unnecessary when you've got adrenaline. Don't think that your skill
or talent alone will carry you through. Chuck that ego out the window,
because—guess what?—everyone there can make at least a few amazing
dishes. And there's one thing I learned from *The Real Housewives of Atlanta*:
"Everyone has a bad day on TV." Just hope that the day your cake doesn't
rise or you drop your crème caramel, someone else screws up even more.

Step 4: Respect Your Competition,
but Never Give Up

This warrants repeating: everyone cast in the show has a chance to win.
Producers want competition, and they see something special in each
contestant, so respect your competition! It does take some luck to come
home with the final W, but never count yourself out. Give it your all, and
never give up.

BREAD

If you're the kind of person who skips the bread chapter in baking books, stop right there! Bread may be a little mysterious, but it's one of the most satisfying things to bake (especially now that stand mixers with dough hooks have made child's play out of kneading dough). Bread's star ingredient, yeast, is actually *alive*, demanding a little extra TLC but paying dividends. Plus, bread is the rare intersection where baking meets practicality. It's a baked good used for sustenance rather than celebration (though it certainly can be festive as well). And as I've said before, bread is the ultimate "come up" metaphor. Like a phoenix rising from the flour-y ashes: Punched down, dough always rises again.

Old-School Dinner Rolls

MAKES 3 DOZEN ROLLS

My Great-Great Aunt Hester perfected these dinner rolls over a century ago. I've updated them using modern appliances so that anyone can make them with ease. These rolls are fluffy and buttery with a hint of sweetness. They bake up next to one another on the pan, and pulling a warm roll off to enjoy straight from the oven is super satisfying.

For additional tips on working with yeast, see page 234.

---

2 cups (480ml) **warm water**

2 large **eggs**

4 tablespoons (55g) **unsalted butter**, melted, plus 6 tablespoons (85g) **unsalted** or **salted butter**

½ cup (100g) **granulated sugar**

2 (¼-ounce/7g) packages **instant yeast**

7 cups (875g) **all-purpose flour**, plus extra as needed

1 tablespoon **kosher salt**

Oil, for the bowl

Flaky sea salt for sprinkling (optional)

---

make ahead Steps 1 and 2 can be done up to 24 hours in advance. Transfer the bowl of dough to the refrigerator, covered, after step 2. The cold air slows the rising process, and a slower rise yields a richer flavor. When ready to bake, remove the dough from the fridge and punch it down before shaping.

1. Add the liquids to the bowl of a stand mixer fitted with the dough hook: the warm water, eggs, and 4 tablespoons melted butter. Then add the dry ingredients: the sugar, yeast, 7 cups flour, and 1 tablepoon salt. Knead on low speed until all the ingredients come together, about 2 minutes. Increase the speed to medium and continue to knead until the dough starts to pull away from the sides of the bowl, 8 to 10 minutes. (It won't form a ball around the hook, and that's okay.)

2. Lightly oil the largest bowl in your kitchen, and transfer the dough to it. The dough will be very sticky. Cover the bowl with plastic wrap or a clean dish towel and let rise until the dough doubles in size, about 1 hour.

3. Melt the remaining 6 tablespoons butter and set aside to allow the butter to cool slightly, but remain melted. (If you've got salted butter, this is a great time to use it.) Line a baking sheet with parchment paper.

4. Use your hands to deflate the risen dough (what we call "punching it down")—really get in there so that no air pockets remain. Tip the dough out onto a floured work surface and roll it to a rectangle 18 by 12 inches—it should be about ½ inch thick. Use a 2½-inch round cutter to stamp out the dough as close together as possible (to minimize the dough scraps). Lightly gather those scraps and pat it into a ½-inch-thick sheet. Stamp out more dough circles until no dough remains. You may need a second baking sheet.

RECIPE CONTINUES

My sister Lucy and I teaching my niece Athena (the next generation!) Aunt Hester's dinner roll recipe

5. This next step requires a little technique. *Lightly* dip both sides of each round in the room-temperature melted butter. You want a thin coat, not a total dunk. (To do this, my mom would melt the butter in a small saucepan and tilt the pan so the butter went to one side, then she'd dip the circle on the other side where there was just a coating of buttery residue.)

6. After being dipped in butter, transfer the circle to the prepared baking sheet. Continue to dip and transfer, lining up the rolls on the baking sheet so they just touch. Be sure to use a light hand—the dough does not like to be handled.

7. Let the dough rise again, until the rolls are puffed up and springy to the touch, 45 minutes to 1 hour, depending on the temperature in your kitchen.

8. Preheat the oven to 400°F and place a rack in the center of the oven. Bake the rolls until the tops are golden brown, about 10 to 14 minutes. Remove the rolls from the oven and brush with melted butter. If you used unsalted butter for finishing, sprinkle the tops lightly with a few pinches of flaky salt; if you used salted butter, skip the additional salt. Serve.

storage These rolls are meltingly delicious straight from the oven, but you can store them by wrapping the room-temperature rolls tightly in foil and freezing them. To reheat frozen rolls, bake in the oven, foil and all, at 400°F until hot. In fact, these freeze so well that my mom has started making the rolls for Thanksgiving a week in advance! It's one less day-of thing to do on her holiday baking checklist.

The Evolution
of Dinner Rolls

My "Old-School" dinner roll recipe has been in my family for *more than 100 years*. The evolution of this recipe may be as fascinating as the ingenuity and resilience of my ancestors who have made the rolls over the years. We call them "Aunt Hester's dinner rolls," but Aunt Hester was actually my great-great-aunt. And it's not a stretch to say that Grandma Leona's maternal aunt is responsible for far more than this recipe; I may very well owe my entire existence to her, since her husband, a physician, probably saved Grandma Leona's life by vaccinating her as an epidemic raged.

My great-grandmother Mattie was Hester's sister. Hester's first husband, Dr. David, was one of the first Black graduates of Indiana University's Medical School. He vaccinated Grandma Leona and her nine siblings, sparing them from the ravaging diphtheria outbreak that took so many lives around them. Grandma Leona had already survived the Spanish flu pandemic that had raged just months after she was born in 1918. But the diphtheria outbreak in her community a decade later proved even more deadly. The family's neighbors and best friends, another family with ten kids, were not as fortunate, and many did not survive the outbreak. Even more devastatingly, Dr. David committed suicide during the Great Depression. But Aunt Hester, a self-sufficient, independent woman who was a college graduate and teacher, kept living. And she kept baking.

When my mom was fourteen years old, she went to Aunt Hester's house and asked her to teach her how to make the dinner rolls that had gained such fame in our close-knit family. "Make 'em up, and make 'em down," was the 1960s roll-making wisdom Aunt Hester imparted to my mother. "Make 'em up" referred to making the dough. Aunt Hester let it slowly ferment in the refrigerator, maximizing the bread's flavor, until she was ready to "make 'em down." This was rolling out the dough, stamping out the rolls, and letting them rise a second time before baking.

Aunt Hester boiled the water, which served as the liquid and was also used to melt the butter (they didn't have microwaves back then). She taught my mom how to dip her finger into the water to determine if it was the Goldilocks temperature for yeast activation: not too hot and not too cold. The last step in "making 'em up" was adding the flour. She added the first 3 cups of flour and used a hand-crank mixer to mix it. Then, she added the final 4 cups and began to knead the dough with her adept hands.

My mom used this method for the next three decades and even passed along the technique to my older sister, Lucy. We always had these dinner rolls for major holidays. But at some point in the '90s, I remember the hand-crank mixer ended up farther and farther in the back of the kitchen drawer; my mom got a stand mixer. It was Lucy who started to add the flour all at once and to use the dough hook on the mixer, forever transforming the way we made these rolls while preserving our joints in a way Aunt Hester could have only dreamed of (she developed debilitating arthritis in her hands).

By the time I got my hands on this recipe (see page 223), I skipped using a measuring cup for the 7 cups of flour (my mom would often forget which cup she was on and have to start over again). Instead, I did the math: 7 cups of all-purpose flour at 125 grams per cup was 875 grams, which I weighed on a scale. Lucy and my mom still boil the water, but I've skipped that, too, opting to melt the butter in the microwave and using instant yeast, which doesn't need warm water to activate it.

Mom would use her wedding champagne flute to stamp out the rolls or sometimes a small mason jar. She would melt butter in a pot, then dip the rolls on the side of the pot to get a perfectly thin coating of butter that wouldn't weigh the dough down from an entire dunk. That butter coating also provided a protective barrier as the rolls rose a second time. I like making the rolls kind of small, because people will definitely want more than one!

My mom, Diane, at age 11 and her cousins Dawn and Linda

Cinnamon Rolls

MAKES 1 DOZEN ROLLS

One year at Thanksgiving, we had some cream cheese frosting left over from making Granny's Million Dollar Cake (page 187). While I was making my Old-School Dinner Rolls (page 223), I went rogue and decided to see if the dinner roll recipe would work for cinnamon rolls. It did! And the pillowy texture and tangy cream cheese icing made them some of the *best* cinnamon rolls I've ever had. But since I can't seem to leave well enough alone, I made a few tweaks: I halved the recipe because cinnamon rolls should be savored. I swapped the warm water for warm milk to make a richer dough, and I added a touch more butter and sugar so that the dough could stand up to the fierce cinnamon filling and delightful cream cheese glaze. The softer your butter is, the easier it will be to spread onto the dough to make the filling. Don't be tempted to melt it—melted butter is more likely to leak through the filling and into the bottom of the pan.

DOUGH

1 cup (240ml) **warm milk**

1 large **egg**

4 tablespoons (55g) **unsalted butter**, melted, plus extra for the bowl and pan

⅓ cup (65g) **granulated sugar**

1 (¼-ounce/7g) package **instant yeast**

3½ cups (420g) **all-purpose flour**, plus extra for rolling and shaping

1½ teaspoons **ground cardamom**

1½ teaspoons **kosher salt**

FILLING

½ cup (1 stick/113g) **unsalted butter**, room temperature

¾ cup (150g) packed **light** or **dark brown sugar**

1 tablespoon **ground cinnamon**

CREAM CHEESE GLAZE

4 tablespoons (55g) **unsalted butter**, room temperature

½ (8-ounce) package (½ cup/113g) **cream cheese**, room temperature

1 cup (125g) **confectioners' sugar**

1 teaspoon **vanilla extract**

make ahead You can make the rolls through step 3. Instead of chilling for 20 minutes, let the dough chill up to 24 hours, covered, in the fridge. The cold air slows the rise of the dough, yielding a richer flavor. When ready to bake, punch the dough down and continue with the recipe.

1. Make the dough: Add the warm milk, egg, and the 4 tablespoons of the melted butter to the bowl of a stand mixer fitted with the dough hook.

2. Add the dry ingredients in the following order: the granulated sugar, yeast, flour, cardamom, and salt. Knead on low speed until the ingredients come together, about 2 minutes. Increase the speed to medium and continue to knead until the dough starts to come away from the sides of the bowl, 8 to 10 minutes (it won't form a ball around the hook).

3. Grease a large bowl with some butter and scrape the dough into it—the dough will be very sticky, but don't worry; as it rests and rises, it will become easier to work with.

RECIPE CONTINUES

Cover the bowl with plastic or a dish towel and let rest until the dough doubles in size, 1 hour to 1 hour 30 minutes. When the dough has doubled in size, set it in the refrigerator for 20 minutes. (This will give the butter a chance to firm up, making it easier to roll out.)

4. Make the filling: In a medium bowl, stir together the softened butter with the brown sugar and cinnamon.

5. Form the rolls: Remove the dough from the refrigerator. Use your fingers to deflate the dough (what we call "punching it down")—really get in there so that no air pockets remain. Use a rubber spatula to scrape the dough onto a generously floured work surface. Roll the dough to an 18 by 14-inch rectangle. (Rolling out bread dough is different from rolling pie dough or cookie dough. Apply very light pressure—there's no need to put your body weight into it. The dough is supple and requires a gentler touch.)

6. Use a spatula to spread the filling over the dough in an even layer, leaving a 1-inch border around the edges. Tightly roll the dough lengthwise from the bottom into a long cylinder. Brush a small amount of water on the last bit of edge and then roll the dough on it to seal (the water is like glue and will help the cylinder stay tight).

7. Cut the cylinder into 12 equal pieces.

8. Grease the bottom of a 9 by 13-inch baking pan. Place the rolls in the pan, making 4 rows of 3 rolls each, setting them an equal distance apart. Cover the pan with plastic or a clean dish towel, and set aside to rise until the rolls have doubled in size and the rolls are touching one another, about 1 hour. (It may seem like these little rolls won't rise that much, but they will. Letting them rise adequately during this step will ensure that they bake up light and fluffy.)

9. Preheat the oven to 400°F and place a rack in the center of the oven. Remove the plastic from the pan and bake until the rolls are puffed up and browned on top, 15 to 20 minutes. Let the rolls cool slightly, in the pan, on a wire rack.

10. While the rolls are baking, make the cream cheese glaze: Add the softened butter, cream cheese, confectioners' sugar, and vanilla to a medium bowl. Use a hand mixer, whisk, or spoon to mix until the glaze is smooth.

11. Spread the glaze over the top of the warm cinnamon rolls and serve warm or at room temperature.

storage Store these, covered, either in the fridge or at room temperature, for up to 4 days.

Challah

MAKES 1 BRAIDED LOAF

Like layering my clothes for cold weather and wearing flats in a city that requires a lot of walking, challah is something New York City introduced me to. Challah is a hallmark of Jewish baking and is traditionally eaten on ceremonial occasions. I love it because it's so versatile. The enriched dough has just enough sweetness to still feel like bread, not dessert. But it's got enough butter and eggs to also be a tender, pillowy treat. (I like to add lemon or orange zest to brighten the flavor.) In fact, I like this enriched dough so much that it became the foundation for one of my favorite festive loaves, Blackberry Lemon King Cake (page 201).

---

1 cup (240ml) **warm water**

3 large **eggs**, room temperature

⅓ cup (65g) **granulated sugar**

1 (¼-ounce/7g) package **instant yeast**

4 cups (500g) **all-purpose flour**, plus more as needed

1½ teaspoons **kosher salt**

5 tablespoons (70g) **unsalted butter**, room temperature

Grated zest from 3 **lemons** (preferably organic)

Softened butter or **vegetable oil**, for the bowl

---

make ahead The dough can be made through step 4 and refrigerated for up to 24 hours. The cold air slows the dough's rise, yielding a richer flavor. When ready to use, remove the dough from the fridge and punch it down before shaping. It will need a little more time on the second rise.

1. Add the warm water and 2 of the eggs to the bowl of a stand mixer fitted with the dough hook.

2. Add the sugar, yeast, flour, salt, the 5 tablespoons of butter, and lemon zest. Knead on low speed until the ingredients have come together, about 2 minutes.

3. Increase the mixer speed to medium and knead until the dough becomes smooth and elastic and the gluten develops, 8 to 10 more minutes. You'll know it's ready when a single ball forms on the dough hook and it thwacks the side of the bowl as the dough hook moves.

4. Remove the bowl from the mixer and shape the dough into a ball. Transfer to a lightly oiled large bowl. Cover the bowl with plastic or a clean damp towel and let rise until it doubles in size, about 1 hour 30 minutes to 2 hours.

5. Line a baking sheet with parchment paper.

6. Use your fingers to deflate the dough (what we call "punching it down")—really get in there so that no air pockets remain. Using a rubber spatula, scrape the dough out onto a lightly floured work surface.

7. Cut the dough into 3 equal pieces and roll each piece into an 18-inch-long rope. Set the ropes parallel to one another on the prepared baking sheet and press the tips of the 3 ropes together at the top; this anchors the dough so you can braid them. Braid the ropes just as you would a ponytail, then press the ends together at the other end and tuck them under.

RECIPE CONTINUES

8. Cover the braided challah with a clean kitchen towel and let it rise until it doubles in size and is spongy to the touch, 45 minutes to 1 hour.

9. Preheat the oven to 350°F and position a rack in the center of the oven. Crack the remaining egg into a small bowl and whisk well. Gently brush the braid with the beaten egg, taking care not to deflate the dough.

10. Transfer the braid to the oven and bake until it's browned on top and sounds hollow when tapped on the side, 30 to 35 minutes. Transfer the baking sheet to a wire rack to cool. You can enjoy this warm, straight from the oven, or let it cool to room temperature.

---

storage Store, covered, at room temperature.

See page 27 for video tutorial instructions on determining gluten development.

A Strength Test for Dough

Gluten is a protein in flour—it is what makes bread chewy. By developing the gluten through kneading, you create a network of strands that trap gas and make the dough stretchy and elastic. You can use a "windowpane" test when kneading to determine if your dough has sufficient gluten development. Hold a small ball of dough in your hands and stretch it apart, creating a windowpane of thin dough. If the dough is elastic enough to stretch so thin that you can see through it without tearing, you know that the gluten can do its miraculous work of making your breads satisfyingly airy and chewy.

Yeast Isn't Scary,
I Promise!

The California Bar Exam and baking-competition-show mystery challenges are things to fear. Yeast, however, is not. These tiny living organisms are just asleep—in a deep sleep. Actually, they're hibernating and it's up to us to gently wake them up so they can make our breads rise to new heights with airy centers! There are just a couple of steps that make it all happen.

Wake Up the Yeast

How we "wake up" the yeast—and whether or not the yeast wakes up at all—is key to fearlessly baking with yeast. In the baking world, we call this "activating" the yeast. There are three types of yeasts: active dry, instant, and fresh.

Active dry yeast: I was raised on this yeast, and it remains a workhorse in my kitchen. I remember watching my mom make Old-School Dinner Rolls (page 223). She'd "wake up" the yeast by heating some water or milk to the Goldilocks temperature—warm enough to get it going, but not so hot that it kills the yeast. The water should be quite warm to the touch, but not *hot*. The goal is between 105° and 115°F, which is a little bit warmer than a baby's bottle. Anything over 120°F will kill the yeast, and dead yeast means dead dough. (Adding salt directly to yeast kills it, too; that's why in most recipes, salt is added to the dough last.) Mom would pour the warm water over the yeast, give it a little stir, then watch and wait for about 10 minutes. Like magic, the motionless yeast would start to bubble up, forming a thick, tannish layer on top. And just like that, the yeast had been awakened from its long slumber.

Instant (rapid rise) yeast: With this yeast you don't need the 10-minute "blooming" period. The yeast granules are smaller, so you don't have to dissolve them in liquid before using them. You add them straight to your mixing bowl with the other dry ingredients and get to kneading. Since you basically get to skip a step of dissolving the yeast in liquid, instant yeast makes breadmaking superefficient. Instant yeast and active dry can be interchanged at a 1:1 ratio.

Fresh yeast (also cake or compressed yeast): This yeast is most often used by professional bakers. It has to be refrigerated and has a short shelf life (just two weeks). It's not that easy to find, but it's easy to use: you just crumble bits of it from the soft semimoist block and mix that in water to activate. A good rule of thumb is to use double the amount of fresh yeast if the recipe calls for active dry or instant yeast. Due to its long shelf life, I prefer active dry or instant yeast.

Proof the Dough

Once your yeast is activated and your dough is made, you can let the dough rise on your counter or overnight in your fridge. My mom would sometimes put the dough near a small pot of simmering water to hurry it along—a warmer environment encourages faster production of gas (which makes the dough puff up). Just don't hurry it too much; dough gets its flavor while it rises, and sometimes a slow rise can be a really good thing. If your kitchen is colder than most, and your dough is moving more slowly than the recipe indicates, just be patient—it will still rise, but it just might take a little longer.

When the dough doubles in size, or "proofs," it's time to knock out all the gas it just burped out. But don't worry—the yeast is not done eating sugar and will continue to produce gas. After you punch the dough down and shape your bread—whether it's dinner rolls or doughnuts—you've got to let it rise one more time. You need to pay closer attention this time, because if you let it rise too much, and the dough is too inflated, the yeast will have spent itself, causing the dough not to rise when it hits the hot oven. One way to double-check the second rise is to touch the dough. It should be springy and bounce back. If you gently press it with a finger and it leaves an imprint, that means the dough needs more time to rise. If the imprint fills in quickly after removing your finger, then it's good to go.

storage Store, covered, at room temperature for up to 3 days. (It will keep longer in the refrigerator or freezer.)

Zulu Babka

MAKES 2 LOAVES

The Krewe of Zulu was always my favorite Mardi Gras Day parade in New Orleans. And snagging a hand-painted coconut was the ultimate prize. The Zulu Social Aid & Pleasure Club, the largest predominantly Black Carnival organization, commissioned a signature king cake from my neighborhood bakery in Baton Rouge, Ambrosia Bakery. Ambrosia's Zulu king cake is filled with cream cheese, chocolate, and coconut—all the best parts of the Zulu parade! This chocolate, cream cheese, and coconut babka is inspired by that king cake, and this delectable blend of ingredients is irresistible!

½ cup (50g) **unsweetened coconut flakes**

1 (8-ounce) package (1 cup/226g) **cream cheese**, room temperature

⅔ cup (80g) **confectioners' sugar**

Dough for Challah (page 231), prepared through step 6

All-purpose flour, for dusting

8 ounces (225g) **semisweet chocolate chips** (preferably mini chocolate chips)

1 large **egg**

2 ounces **dark chocolate,** melted (optional)

1. Preheat the oven to 350°F. Line each of two 9 by 5-inch loaf pans with a strip of parchment paper, leaving some overhang so you can easily lift the loaves from the pans.

2. Spread the coconut flakes on a baking sheet in a single layer and toast in the oven until lightly browned, 5 to 7 minutes.

3. In a small bowl, stir the cream cheese and confectioners' sugar together until combined.

4. Use a rolling pin to gently roll the risen bread dough into a 16 by 8-inch rectangle on a lightly floured surface. The dough is supple and requires only a gentle touch.

5. Use a rubber spatula to spread the cream cheese mixture over the dough in an even layer, leaving a 1-inch border around the edges. Then sprinkle with the chocolate chips and half of the coconut flakes (save the remaining to sprinkle on top).

6. Tightly roll the dough lengthwise, starting from the bottom, until it is a tight cylinder. Brush a little water along the top edge and press it to close the cylinder; the water is like glue and will seal the edge.

7. Cut the cylinder in half crosswise so that you have 2 shorter pieces. Cut each piece in half lengthwise through the center, exposing the filling. Now, twist the 2 halves together and transfer a twist to each prepared loaf pan. Let the dough proof, covered with plastic or a dish towel, until doubled in size, about 1 hour.

8. Preheat the oven to 350°F and place a rack in the middle of the oven.

9. Whisk the egg in a small bowl. Brush the loaves with egg wash and bake until nicely browned, about 30 minutes.

10. Let the pans cool on a wire rack until the loaves are cooled to room temperature. Then, remove the loaves from the pans, drizzle the tops with melted chocolate (if desired), and sprinkle with the remaining coconut before serving.

Hot Skillet Cornbread

MAKES ONE 10-INCH CORNBREAD

When I was growing up, we always kept those little blue and white boxes of Jiffy corn muffin mix in the pantry. The muffins were easy enough to make—just add an egg and a little milk, give it a good stir, and pour the batter into a muffin tin for 6 rounded little cornbread muffins. We had dinner one evening with a family friend, Ms. Marsha Gilbeaux. Ms. Marsha cooked differently from my mom. She was the kind of mom who "doctored up" foods. She added an extra egg and a little sugar to the Jiffy cornbread mix!

Ms. Marsha's cornbread was a revelation. So, I started "doctoring up" cornbread myself—using buttermilk instead of regular milk and adding creamed corn—and finally, making it from scratch. And as flavorful as this new version is, the best part is the crunchy, almost-caramelized edges of nearly fried cornbread, thanks to pouring the batter into a hot skillet of sizzling butter. Gone are those rounded little corn muffins, as cute as they were.

½ cup (1 stick/113g) **unsalted butter,** plus extra for serving

1½ cups (180g) **cornmeal** (fine or medium grind)

1 cup (125g) **all-purpose flour**

½ cup (100g) **granulated sugar**

2 teaspoons **baking powder**

1½ teaspoons **kosher salt**

½ teaspoon **baking soda**

3 large **eggs**

1 cup (240ml) **buttermilk** (see page 51)

½ cup canned **creamed corn**

1. Preheat the oven to 375°F and place a rack in the middle of the oven. Add the butter to a 10-inch cast-iron skillet, and place it in the oven. You're both heating the skillet and melting the butter.

2. In a large bowl, whisk together the cornmeal, flour, sugar, baking powder, salt, and baking soda. Add the eggs and buttermilk and whisk until combined. Stir in the creamed corn.

3. Carefully remove the skillet from the oven. The butter should be completely melted, and some of the milk solids might even be browned. Pour about three-fourths of the melted butter into the cornmeal batter and stir until combined (leave the remaining butter in the skillet). The batter will start to look smooth when the melted butter is fully incorporated.

4. Pour the batter into the hot skillet. The melted butter may form a little ring around the batter, and that is a good thing because that will ensure there's a nicely browned crust around the cornbread.

5. Bake until the cornbread is browned around the edges and a toothpick inserted in the center comes out clean, 20 to 25 minutes. Remove from the oven and serve hot with a slather of butter.

---

storage Store, covered, at room temperature for 3 days. (The cornbread will keep even longer in the refrigerator or freezer.)

Brioche

MAKES 1 TOWERING LOAF

You know how some people have book clubs? Well, my mom and I share a bread club. We pick a recipe every few weeks and then make it at the same time—a perfect way to have some long-distance mother-daughter time. The idea was born during a trip to Paris together, when we attended a "traditional" Viennoisserie and bread-making class at Le Cordon Bleu. Our favorite bread to bake was and still is brioche.

Brioche is an "enriched" dough. This means it has additional fat, sugar, eggs, and dairy. Indeed, a seemingly impossible amount of butter is crammed into this dough, and all that butter makes this bread meltingly light and super flavorful. In fact, there's so much butter in it that you will have to stand over the mixer as it kneads, sturdy spatula in hand, helping the reluctant solid butter to incorporate into the dough.

I assure you, brioche is worth all that butter! The dough is special also in that she likes to take her time to get ready, and she needs a lot of beauty rest in the fridge. (This extended six-hour "beauty sleep" is *not* optional!) If you follow these directions, you will have one stunningly tall, proudly buttery loaf of brioche to enjoy warm from the oven, or as the perfect slice for French toast the following morning.

---

6 large **eggs**

¼ cup (60ml) **whole milk**

6 tablespoons (75g) **granulated sugar**

1 (¼-ounce/7g) package **active dry yeast** (see page 234)

4 cups (500g) **bread flour**, plus extra as needed

2 teaspoons **kosher salt**

1 cup (2 sticks/226g) **unsalted butter**, plus extra as needed

1. Combine 5 of the eggs, the milk, sugar, yeast, flour, and salt in the bowl of a stand mixer fitted with the dough hook. Knead on low speed until the ingredients come together, about 3 minutes (see Notes, page 242). The dough will be dry and stiff—use a rubber spatula to make sure all the flour at the bottom of the bowl gets incorporated. Turn the mixer off and let the dough rest for 10 minutes. This gives the dough a chance to hydrate.

2. Remove the butter from the refrigerator and wrap in plastic. Pound it with a rolling pin so that it's flattened and pliable. Break the butter into 1-inch pieces.

3. Turn the mixer to medium-high speed and knead the dough until the gluten develops and the dough comes together in a ball on the dough hook, 10 to 12 minutes; it will thwack the sides of the bowl as the dough hook moves. (You may need to stop the mixer occasionally to scrape the bottom and sides of the bowl if all the dough is not being kneaded.)

4. With the mixer on low speed, add the butter a few small pieces at a time until it is all incorporated, about 3 minutes. If the chunks of butter creep up the side of the bowl and are out of reach of the dough hook, you'll have to help it along by stopping the mixer and using a rubber spatula to scoot the butter back down into the bottom of the bowl.

5. When the butter is all incorporated, increase the speed to medium and knead (see Notes, page 242) until smooth and the dough

RECIPE CONTINUES

comes together in a single mass on the dough hook, 10 to 12 more minutes. (During this kneading, you will likely need to stop your machine several times to scrape the bottom and sides of the bowl.) Eventually the very loose dough will come together and thwack the sides of the bowl. Now, it's ready.

6. Turn the mixer off and remove the bowl from the stand. Cover the bowl with plastic or a clean dish towel and let rest at room temperature for 30 minutes.

7. Use a little butter to grease a large bowl. Use a rubber spatula to scrape the dough out onto a floured work surface, and use both hands to roll it into a tight ball. Place the ball of dough in the bowl, seam side down, and refrigerate, covered, for at least 6 hours and up to 48 hours.

8. The dough will have risen into a beautiful ball. When you touch it, it will feel solid, which is different from other risen doughs. This is because all that butter solidified in the refrigerator. Punch the dough down and transfer it to a floured work surface. You will have about 2¼ pounds of dough.

9. Smear softened butter in a 9 by 5-inch loaf pan. Divide the dough into 3 equal pieces; Shape each into a ball. Place them side by side in the prepared pan, loosely cover with a kitchen towel, and let rise until the loaf pan looks crowded because the dough has expanded to touch all sides of the pan and has risen over the edge. The properly proofed dough will feel soft and springy when lightly touched. This second proofing will take

between 1½ and 2 hours, depending on how warm the room is.

10. Preheat the oven to 350°F and place a rack in the center of the oven.

11. Place the remaining egg in a small bowl and whisk. Gently brush the top of the loaf with the egg wash, then use a sharp knife to cut a 1-inch-deep line lengthwise down the center of the loaf.

12. Transfer the loaf pan to the oven and bake until the aroma of warm buttery bread blesses your kitchen, the loaf has risen several inches above the pan, and it is a rich golden brown, 40 to 45 minutes. Transfer to a cooling rack and let rest in the pan for 10 minutes before removing from the pan to cool completely. Serve warm, by the slice.

---

storage Store leftover brioche in an airtight container in the refrigerator for up to 1 week. This bread makes excellent toast.

---

notes Since the brioche will rest in the refrigerator for an extended time, you don't have to first activate the yeast by adding it to warm liquid. You want a slower rise, so the lower-temperature liquids will sufficiently wake up the yeast.

Be sure your stand mixer doesn't overheat during the kneading—this heavy work can cause some mixers to stop. Just touch the machine and make sure it isn't getting hot. If it is, turn it off and give it a break for 5 minutes, then get back to kneading.

NYC Bagels

MAKES 8 BAGELS

New York City bagels have a crisp exterior that gives way to a wonderful chewy interior with each bite. Bagels are usually slathered with copious amounts of cream cheese, but if you want to splurge, there is no better breakfast (or lunch) than a bagel with lox (or smoked salmon), cream cheese, capers, a thick tomato slice, and some rings of red onion. To me, the coolest thing about bagels is that they're a boil-then-bake bread. You actually boil the rings of dough prior to baking, which sets the crust!

1¼ cups (300ml) **warm water**

1 teaspoon **active dry yeast** (see page 234)

4 cups (500g) **bread flour**, plus extra as needed

4 tablespoons (80g) **honey** or **barley malt syrup** (see Note, page 244)

1 tablespoon (12g) **granulated sugar**

4 teaspoons **kosher salt**

Unsalted butter, room temperature, for the baking sheet

1 tablespoon **baking soda**

Poppy seeds, **sesame seeds**, or **everything bagel seasoning** (optional)

Cream cheese and other toppings (optional)

1. Add ½ cup of the warm water to the bowl of a stand mixer fitted with the dough hook. Add the yeast and dissolve, using a fork or whisk. Let stand until cloudy, about 10 minutes.

2. Add the remaining warm water, bread flour, 2 tablespoons of the honey, the sugar, and 2 teaspoons of the salt. Knead on low speed until the ingredients come together, about 2 minutes. Increase the speed to medium-high and continue to knead; you may need to stop the mixer and push the dough down with a spatula occasionally. The dough should be dry but sticky. After 10 minutes, do the windowpane test (see page 232) to make sure the gluten has developed.

3. Cover the bowl with plastic or a clean dish towel and let the dough rest for 1 hour. It won't double in size, and that's okay; the dough should spring back if you gently apply pressure with your fingertips.

4. Line a baking sheet with parchment paper and grease it with a little butter. Set a cooling rack atop a second baking sheet.

5. Tip the dough out onto a lightly floured work surface and divide it into 8 equal pieces—about 105 grams each if you are using a scale. Roll each piece into a ball. Poke through the center of each ball and stretch the center to form a 2-inch hole. Cover the bagels on the sheet with plastic or a clean towel and let rest for an additional 25 minutes.

RECIPE CONTINUES

6. Preheat the oven to 425°F and place a rack in the top third of the oven.

7. Fill a large pot (an 8-quart works great, but a smaller one will be fine, too) about two-thirds full with water. Add the remaining 2 teaspoons salt, the remaining 2 tablespoons honey, and the baking soda. Bring the water to a boil, then reduce the heat so it's at a hearty simmer.

8. Carefully drop the bagels into the water a few at a time, boiling 1 minute on one side, using a spoon or skewer to flip them over, then boiling an additional minute on the other side. Use a slotted spoon to carefully remove them from the water and place on the cooling rack. If you are using toppings, such as poppy seeds, sprinkle on top while the bagels are wet and sticky.

9. Line a clean baking sheet with parchment paper. Bake the bagels until browned, 20 to 25 minutes. Transfer the bagels to the cooling rack and let cool for 30 minutes. (The insides of the bagels continue to cook as they cool.)

10. When ready to serve, use a bread knife or other sharp knife to slice the bagels in half. Toast if you like and top with seasonings and spreads, if desired.

---

storage Store, covered, at room temperature for up to 2 days.

---

note Purists will tell you that bagels must be made with barley malt syrup, which will yield a shinier crust. But I'm more likely to have honey on hand, which works just fine. It's used in both the dough and the water for boiling.

DOUGHNUTS
& other fried things

I will drive 30 minutes across town for a good doughnut, then immediately after devouring it I'll begin to obsess about getting my next fix. Making doughnuts at home adds an extra dimension: you can enjoy them hot, super fresh, and as fanciful and flavorful as you desire. Some bakers may think that homemade doughnuts are intimidating, but I've discovered that the trick is all in how you fry 'em. Here's everything you need to know to master those elusive doughnuts: how to make, fry, glaze, and fill. And I'll walk you step-by-step through "one of the best doughnuts I've ever had!" (Paul Hollywood's words, not mine!)

Basic Doughnut Recipe (That's Anything but Basic)

MAKES 1 DOZEN DOUGHNUTS

Making successful doughnuts requires three things: following the rules for yeast-raised breads; creating a delicious flavor; and sticking to techniques for proper frying (see page 258). After testing batches and batches of doughnuts, I developed this recipe, an adaptation of the pillowy-soft Berliner, a doughnut that is traditionally filled with jam, but when left plain makes for an excellent glazed doughnut.

¾ cup plus 2 tablespoons (200ml) **whole milk**, warmed but not hot

6 tablespoons (85g) **unsalted butter**, melted and room temperature, plus softened butter for the bowl

1 large **egg** plus 2 large **egg yolks**, room temperature

3 cups (375g) **all-purpose flour**, plus more as needed

1 cup (125g) **bread flour**

1 (¼-ounce/7g) package **instant yeast**

¼ cup (50g) **granulated sugar**

1 teaspoon **kosher salt**

Grated zest from 2 **oranges** (about 2 tablespoons)

Vegetable oil, for frying

Granulated sugar or **glaze of choice** (optional)

1. Add the milk, 6 tablespoons melted butter, the egg and egg yolks, 3 cups all-purpose flour, the bread flour, yeast, sugar, salt, and orange zest to the bowl of a stand mixer fitted with the dough hook. Knead on low speed until the ingredients come together, about 2 minutes. Increase the speed to medium-low and continue to knead until the dough is smooth and elastic, about 10 minutes more.

2. Lightly grease a large bowl with the softened butter. Tip the dough out of the stand mixer into the prepared bowl. Cover the bowl with plastic or a clean dish towel and set aside in a draft-free area until the dough has doubled in size, about 1 hour. You may need more or less time depending on how warm or cold your kitchen is.

3. Remove the plastic wrap and use your fingers to deflate the dough so no air pockets remain. (The goal here is just to deflate the dough and remove the air—save the aggressive punching down for a kickboxing class!) With the dough still in the bowl, fold it into 3 parts, like a letter. Then, turn the dough over and place the plastic wrap back on the bowl. Allow the dough to rise a second time, until doubled again in size. (This will be a much quicker rise—about 45 minutes.)

4. Tip the dough out onto a floured work surface. Use your hands to gently pat it down to about ¾-inch thickness, trying to retain as much air as possible. Use a floured cutter to cut the doughnut shapes, using a

RECIPE CONTINUES

much smaller cutter, bottle cap, or the tip of a wooden spoon to cut out the center hole (except for cream-filled doughnuts).

5. Lightly flour 2 baking sheets. Place the doughnuts on the prepared sheets, leaving at least 4 inches of space between them. Cover with plastic until they have doubled in size and look like they're about to pop, about 30 minutes (the rising time depends on how warm your kitchen is).

6. Line a baking sheet with paper towels. Add enough oil to a Dutch oven, deep pot, or deep-fry pot to a depth of at least 2 inches and heat until the oil reaches 325°F on a thermometer (see Note).

7. Carefully drop up to 3 doughnuts at a time into the hot oil so you don't overcrowd the pan and cook until golden brown, 1 minute to 1 minute 15 seconds. Use a slotted spoon to flip the doughnuts and cook until the other side is golden brown, about 1 minute more. Transfer the doughnuts to the paper towel–lined baking sheet. Let the oil return to 325°F, then fry the remaining doughnuts.

8. Dip the warm doughnuts in granulated sugar or glaze to coat before enjoying.

---

note Having a thermometer is essential for deep-frying these doughnuts. See tips for frying on page 258.

How I Learned to Make Doughnuts

As a child, I was lured countless times by the glowing red "Hot Doughnuts Now" sign. Those perfect rings of dough would glide down the conveyor belt and were showered with waterfalls of sugary glaze. They were then rescued with tongs, packed into a box, and ushered into my hands. The warm dough and sugar melded into one, melting in my mouth. Those cloyingly sweet doughnuts made my face pucker. I'd reach for another; it was easy to eat more than one.

Naturally, I tried making my own, but my experiments all came out heavy and oil laden. When doughnut pans came on the scene, I was hopeful, yet skeptical. Sure, baking would solve my frying misgivings, but doughnuts baked in ring-shaped pans tasted and felt more like muffins. Proper doughnuts are *fried* with a thin and crispy exterior and pillowy insides.

Imagine how horrified I was to learn that the signature recipe for episode 2 of *The Great American Baking Show* was none other than doughnuts! I had never made a *good* batch of doughnuts, so how was I going to make a *great* batch? With just a few days to submit my recipe, I got to frying.

Over the course of a long August weekend, while my friends ventured out to the beach at Jacob Riis Park on Long Island to toss around Frisbees and sip rum punch, I stayed home, leaning over a vat of hot oil as drops of sweat from my face bounced in, ricocheting off of the oil. Everything that could go wrong did. Some doughnuts were dense. Others were burnt on the outside and raw on the inside. Still others were heavy with oil. Plus, the flavor was okay, but nothing special. I wasn't about to let doughnuts take me out in just the second episode of the show, so I cranked up my resolve.

The lack of air-conditioning in my New York apartment finally paid off. It was hot and steamy—98°F, according to my candy thermometer—which was just the environment my dough needed to rise quickly, mimicking the humidity of the proofing drawer I would have access to during the challenge.

With each failed batch, I learned a lesson. When doughnuts come out dense, it means they need to be proofed longer. To maintain that perfect doughnut shape, I learned to lower them delicately into the hot oil. To cook them to a perfect golden-brown with an airy interior, the oil needs to be regulated—not too hot, not to cool (and not too many doughnuts at once!). The flavor of my doughnut dough improved when I added fresh orange zest, the perfect punch of tart flavor to balance the sweetness from the glaze. Eventually, I got the hang of it and mastered the details that go into making the most deliciously memorable doughnuts. And it all paid off—my Tiger Doughnuts (opposite) earned me a Hollywood handshake and the title of Star Baker that week!

Tiger Doughnuts

MAKES 1 DOZEN DOUGHNUTS

These light, airy doughnuts are bursting with citrus flavor complemented with a drizzle of milk chocolate. There's orange zest in the dough as well as in the glaze. There's also orange juice and orange liqueur in the glaze, which really dials up the flavor. And the texture is as good as the flavor—proof them properly, and these doughnuts will be feather light.

2 cups (250g) **confectioners' sugar**

Grated zest from 1 **orange** (about 1 tablespoon), plus 2 tablespoons (30ml) **orange juice**

2 tablespoons (30ml) **orange liqueur**

All-purpose flour, for sprinkling

Dough for Basic Doughnut Recipe (page 249), prepared through step 3

Vegetable oil, for frying

3 ounces **milk chocolate**, finely chopped

storage If you go through the trouble of making homemade doughnuts, enjoy them in all their warm, sugary glory and eat them just as soon as they're done. But if you must wait, these will keep for the day since they are coated with glaze, which helps lock in the freshness.

1. Whisk the confectioners' sugar, orange zest and juice, and orange liqueur in a small bowl until you have a creamy glaze.

2. Generously sprinkle 2 baking sheets with flour. Set the doughnut dough on a lightly floured surface and pat into a rectangle about ¾ inch thick. Use a pizza slicer to cut the doughnuts into 2½-inch squares. Use a 1-inch round cutter or bottle cap to cut the holes from the middles (by making square doughnuts, there are no scraps to deal with—just doughnut holes). Transfer the doughnuts to the prepared baking sheets, leaving 4 inches between them so they won't touch and stick together as they rise. Cover with plastic wrap or a clean dish towel and let the doughnuts rise until puffy and doubled in size, about 40 minutes.

3. Prepare an assembly line: the baking sheets with the uncooked doughnuts, a baking sheet lined with paper towels, and a cooling rack set on top of a sheet pan. Set the bowl of glaze next to the cooling rack

4. Add oil to a Dutch oven or large pot to a depth of at least 2 inches and heat. When the oil reaches 325°F on an instant-read thermometer, add the doughnuts 3 at a time and fry until golden brown on both sides, 1 minute to 1 minute 15 seconds per side, flipping just once. Use a slotted spoon to transfer the doughnuts to the paper towel–lined baking sheet. Check the temperature of the oil frequently; when it returns to 325°F, add the next batch of doughnuts.

RECIPE CONTINUES

5. Meanwhile, glaze the first 3 doughnuts while they're still hot. Set a doughnut into the bowl of glaze, and use skewers or chopsticks to flip the doughnut over to glaze the other side. Lift the doughnut out with a skewer by the hole in the middle and allow the excess glaze to drip off before setting the doughnut, pretty side up, on the cooling rack. (Setting the glazed doughnuts on the rack allows the glaze to drip down without pooling at the bottom of the doughnut.) Repeat until all the doughnuts are fried and glazed.

6. Melt the chocolate in the microwave in 30-second intervals. Use a spoon to drizzle chocolate on top of each doughnut. Admire your handiwork before devouring and sharing.

VARIATION

Puckery Lemon Doughnuts
Follow the recipe for Tiger Doughnuts but use 1 tablespoon lemon zest in place of the orange zest and ⅓ cup (60ml) fresh lemon juice in place of the orange juice and liqueur. Skip the chocolate drizzle.

Air-Fried Doughnuts

You can "fry" doughnuts in your air fryer! Cook at 325° F, 2 to 3 minutes per side. The texture is spongier, but they're still delicious!

Chocolate Cream-Filled Doughnuts

MAKES 10 DOUGHNUTS

These doughnuts are filled with chocolate pastry cream. The cream filling must be prepared at least 2 hours in advance so it has time to cool. Coat with glaze or simply roll in granulated sugar.

⅓ cup (80ml) **heavy cream**

½ recipe **Chocolate pastry cream** (see page 277), chilled

All-purpose flour, for the baking sheets

Dough for Basic Doughnut Recipe (page 249), prepared through step 3

Creamy Vanilla Glaze (page 276), or granulated sugar

Vegetable oil, for frying

1. Place the heavy cream in the bowl of a stand mixer fitted with the whisk attachment (or in a medium bowl and use a hand mixer). Whisk or beat on medium speed until you have medium peaks. Fold in the pastry cream until smooth. Transfer to a piping bag with a large tip and give the top of the bag a twist to prevent air from entering. Let the filling chill in the refrigerator for 2 hours.

2. Lightly flour 2 baking sheets.

3. Pat the risen doughnut dough to ¾ inch thick. Use a round 2½-inch cutter to stamp out the doughnuts. Transfer them to the baking sheets, giving them space to rise so they won't touch and stick together. (It's important that the surface is floured so that they don't stick to the sheet.) Cover with plastic wrap or a clean dish towel and let rise until puffy, bloated, and doubled in size, about 45 minutes.

4. Prepare an assembly line: the baking sheets of risen doughnuts, a baking sheet lined with paper towels, and a cooling rack set on a sheet pan. The bowl of glaze can sit next to the cooling rack. Add oil to a Dutch oven or large pot to a depth of at least 2 inches and heat. When the oil reaches 325°F, fry the doughnuts 3 at a time for 60 to 75 seconds per side, flipping just once. When the doughnuts are golden on both sides, transfer them to the paper towel–lined baking sheet. Check the temperature of the oil; if it's back to 325°F, add the next batch of doughnuts and repeat.

5. Meanwhile, glaze the first 3 doughnuts. Dip each one in the glaze, individually. Use chopsticks or skewers to turn the doughnut over. When fully coated, lift the doughnut out with a skewer to allow the glaze to drip off. Then, place the glazed doughnut, pretty side up, on the cooling rack. Repeat until all the doughnuts are fried and glazed. Allow the doughnuts to cool completely, about 30 minutes.

6. Fill the doughnuts by inserting the piping tip of the pastry bag into the side of the doughnut and giving a steady squeeze of the filling until the doughnut feels heavy—2 to 3 tablespoons of cream per doughnut. Enjoy immediately.

storage Let the doughnuts cool completely, then store in an airtight container for up to 2 days.

Fry Doughnuts
Like a Pro

Proper frying is the key to achieving doughnut perfection. Pay attention to two things: temperature and time. To measure temperature, a thermometer is a must. I like a clip-on candy thermometer or instant-read thermometer. To measure time, I like to use the stopwatch on my cell phone or the timer on my microwave.

Smaller doughnuts and doughnut holes fry more quickly than larger doughnuts. For every doughnut, there is a Goldilocks temperature range. If the oil is too hot, the doughnut will burn on the outside and not be fully cooked on the inside. If the oil is too cold, the doughnut will absorb excess grease as it cooks, since it has to stay in the oil longer to cook through. Pay attention to the temperatures listed in the recipes, and for best results, check the temperature of the oil regularly.

The oil temperature will fluctuate, but there are a few tricks for regulating it. First, check the temperature of the oil not only before frying your first batch but also between batches. If the oil is too hot, add some room-temperature oil, which will cool it down. You can also fry some scraps or doughnut holes, since frying cools down the oil, too (and offers a snack for the baker!). Or simply turn the heat down (or completely off). If the oil isn't hot enough, crank up the heat and be patient—wait until it's in the right temperature range before adding more doughnuts.

Measuring time is much easier. Pay attention to the time ranges given in the recipes, but also use your senses. A doughnut is ready when it's a light golden brown. If it took you 1 minute 15 seconds to get one side golden brown, then use your timer, starting at zero, for the other side after you've flipped the doughnut. No matter what you're frying, always test the first couple to make sure they're cooked inside.

Here are some additional points: After frying, the oil can be reused a few more times. I filter it through a strainer lined with cheesecloth, then funnel it right back into its container.

When working with hot oil, it's necessary to take proper precautions. Wear shoes that cover your feet entirely, long pants, a shirt that doesn't expose your chest, and long sleeves; these items will protect you if the oil splatters. You can also protect your hands by wearing an oven mitt.

Old-Fashioned Doughnuts

MAKES 8 DOUGHNUTS

While I love the pillowy insides of yeast-raised doughnuts, I also love the texture of old-fashioned cake doughnuts. The batter for these ridged glazed doughnuts is prepared just like cake batter: Cream butter and sugar together, beat in the eggs, then add the flour mixture, alternating with the wet ingredients. The key to easily rolling out and handling the dough is to keep it cold. Then you fry 'em just like you would any other doughnut. They aren't greasy or heavy, and the tang from the sour cream makes the perfect taste and crumbly texture.

2½ cups (250g) **cake flour**, plus extra as needed

1½ teaspoons **baking powder**

1 teaspoon **kosher salt**

½ cup (100g) **granulated sugar**

2 tablespoons (28g) **unsalted butter**, room temperature

2 large **egg** yolks

⅔ cup (160g) **sour cream**

Vegetable oil, for the bowl and for frying

Creamy Vanilla Glaze (page 276)

See page 27 for video tutorial instructions on frying doughnuts.

1. Combine the dry ingredients. Sift the cake flour and baking powder into a large bowl. Whisk in the salt, then set aside.

2. In the bowl of a stand mixer fitted with the paddle attachment, beat the sugar and butter on medium-low speed until smooth and creamy, about 1 minute.

3. Add the egg yolks and increase the speed to medium. Continue to beat until the ingredients are well combined, about 1 minute, scraping the sides and bottom of the bowl as needed.

4. Reduce the mixer speed to low. Add ⅓ of the flour mixture. Mix on low speed until just combined, then add half the sour cream and mix on low speed until just combined. Repeat, adding half of the remaining flour mixture, followed by the remaining sour cream, and finally the remaining flour mixture, combining until no streaks of flour remain. Stop the mixer to scrape the sides and bottom of the bowl as needed.

5. Lightly oil a large bowl and transfer the dough to the bowl. Cover the bowl with plastic wrap and refrigerate for 1 hour so the butter can firm up.

6. Generously flour a baking sheet. Flour a large piece of wax paper and tip out the dough onto the wax paper (it will be sticky!). Generously flour the top of the dough and place a second piece of wax paper on top. Roll out the dough until it is ½ to ¾ inch thick. Carefully remove the top piece of wax paper. (If the wax paper sticks, use more flour next

RECIPE CONTINUES

time.) Generously coat a 2½-inch doughnut cutter with flour. Cut out the doughnuts, coating the cutter with flour between each cut. Use a spatula to carefully move the doughnuts to the floured baking sheet. Gently brush off any excess flour on each doughnut. Gather the scraps, gently knead, and repeat.

7. Line a plate with paper towels. Place a cooling rack on a baking sheet lined with parchment paper.

8. Heat 2 inches of oil in a Dutch oven or large pot for deep-frying. When the oil reaches 325°F, gently place 3 doughnuts into the oil (the doughnuts need plenty of room to bob around). They will immediately sink and then should rise to the surface. When they rise, gently flip them over using a skewer, chopstick, or butter knife. Fry until they are golden, 2 to 3 minutes, then flip and fry on the other side until golden, another 2 to 3 minutes. Transfer the doughnuts to the rack set over the baking sheet to drain for about 1 minute.

9. While they're still hot, submerge the ridged top-side of each doughnut into the glaze and place on the cooling rack, glazed side up. Repeat until all the doughnuts have been fried and glazed. Serve immediately.

---

storage Let the doughnuts cool completely, then store in an airtight container for up to 2 days.

Beignet Fingers

SERVES 8

It was a short journey through the familiar landscape of Central Park, but the culmination of a much longer journey for me: my first live cooking segment debut for a major TV network and on a major show—ABC's *The Chew*. I'd be going on air in front of millions of people *live* to make beignets with my food TV idol, Carla Hall!

It had been more than six months since the unceremonious disappearance of *The Great American Baking Show*. Yet through a series of events—from giving an interview on CNN, to recording the *Speaking Broadly* podcast with former *Food & Wine* editor in chief Dana Cowin, to a talent booker for the Hallmark Channel listening to that podcast and inviting me to Los Angeles—I was still, miraculously, on people's radar.

Backstage, I counseled myself: *Relax! Have fun! You got this!* When I got onto the set, with Carla Hall to my left (!) and Clinton Kelly to my right, I was pumped with adrenaline. Carla and Clinton were clearly enjoying themselves, and it was infectious—not only did I join in but I even found myself dancing as we came back from the commercial break!

This is that same beignet batter, just in a different shape, echoing the beignet fingers my friends and I would order when we'd meet up at Coffee Call in Baton Rouge. We'd order the beignet fingers along with mugs of café au lait mixed with hot chocolate. I like serving them the same way—on a giant plate so everyone gets to dig in.

1 (¼-ounce/7g) package **instant yeast**

¾ cup **warm water**

⅓ cup (65g) **granulated sugar**

½ cup (120ml) **evaporated milk**

1 large **egg**

½ teaspoon **kosher salt**

3½ cups (420g) **all-purpose flour**, plus extra for shaping

2 tablespoons (30g) **unsalted butter**, melted

Vegetable oil, for frying

Confectioners' sugar

---

1. To the bowl of a stand mixer fitted with the dough hook, add the yeast, warm water, granulated sugar, evaporated milk, egg, salt, 3½ cups flour, and melted butter. Knead on low speed until the ingredients have come together, about 2 minutes. Increase the speed to medium-low and continue to knead until the dough is smooth and elastic, 8 to 10 minutes.

2. Remove the bowl from the stand mixer. Cover the bowl with plastic wrap or a clean dish towel and set aside in a draft-free area to rise until the dough has doubled in size, about 1 hour 30 minutes.

3. Use your fingers to deflate the dough—really get in there to punch it down so there are no air pockets.

4. In a Dutch oven or large pot, add enough oil to be 4 inches deep, and heat to 370°F.

RECIPE CONTINUES

5. Tip the dough out onto a heavily floured work surface, sprinkle flour on the top of the dough, and use a rolling pin to roll it ¼ inch thick, sprinkling additional flour on top and beneath the dough as needed. Use a sharp knife or pizza slicer to cut the dough into strips that are ½ to 1 inch wide and 4 to 5 inches long. They don't have to be perfectly uniform!

6. Line a baking sheet with paper towels. Carefully lower 5 or 6 strips into the hot oil and use a slotted spoon to flip the strips every 15 to 20 seconds, until they are golden brown on both sides, about 2 minutes total. Use a slotted spoon to transfer the strips to the baking sheet. Repeat with the remaining dough strips, making sure the oil returns to 370°F between batches, until all the beignet fingers are fried.

7. Pile the fingers on a small plate and dust generously with confectioners' sugar. These are best served hot, straight from the fryer.

Fried Hand Pies

MAKES 10 HAND PIES

These crescent-shaped hand pies have shortening in the crust because shortening has a lower melting point than butter. This means the crust has a chance to cook and flake up when it hits the hot oil. The buttermilk gives a tangy boost of flavor while adding to the flakiness, and the egg and sugar encourage the little pies to brown and become a gorgeous amber color. The balance of textures creates a symphony with each bite—flaky on the outside and warm, gooey pie filling on the inside.

2¼ cups (270g) **all-purpose flour**, plus extra for the work surface

1 tablespoon (12g) **granulated sugar**

½ teaspoon **kosher salt**

½ cup (113g) **shortening**, cut into 1-inch pieces

½ cup (120ml) **buttermilk** (see page 51)

1 large **egg**

1 cup (120g) **canned pie filling of choice**

Vegetable oil, for frying

¼ cup (50g) **granulated sugar** mixed with 2 teaspoons **ground cinnamon** (optional)

storage The hand pies will keep in an airtight container at room temperature for up to 3 days.

1. In a large bowl (or in the bowl of a food processor), whisk together 2¼ cups flour, the sugar, and salt (or pulse to combine). Add the shortening and use a pastry blender to cut the shortening into the flour until it is pea size (or pulse the mixture until the pieces of shortening are pea size).

2. In a small bowl, whisk together the buttermilk and egg. Pour it over the flour mixture. Use a large spoon to stir until you have a shaggy dough.

3. Tip out the contents of the bowl onto a floured work surface. Flatten the dough, then fold it in half on top of itself. Flatten again and repeat this 3 times (this helps incorporate any bits of flour while also making tons of flaky layers). Wrap the dough in plastic and refrigerate for at least 1 hour.

4. Roll out the dough on a floured work surface to a ⅛-inch thickness. Use a 4-inch round cutter to cut out 10 circles of dough. Spoon about a tablespoon of pie filling into the center of each round, leaving about a 1-inch border. Lightly brush a little water around the bottom half of the filling, fold in half, and use a fork to seal the edges of the pastry.

5. Line a baking sheet with paper towels. Heat 3 inches of oil in a Dutch oven or large pot for deep-frying. When the oil reaches 350°F, carefully lower 2 or 3 pies into the oil and fry until golden all over, 2 to 3 minutes. Transfer the pies to the baking sheet to drain and repeat with the remaining hand pies.

6. Dip both sides of each pie in the cinnamon-sugar mixture, if desired, and serve warm.

Hushpuppies

MAKES 2½ DOZEN SMALL HUSHPUPPIES

Hushpuppies are essentially fried cornbread. (Can you think of anything tastier!?) They're deceptively easy to make. In Louisiana, we serve these as a side with just about any meal, but they are pretty much mandatory if you're having fried seafood.

When I was growing up in Baton Rouge, my family would go to Ralph & Kacoo's (a Cajun seafood restaurant) every Sunday after church. The paper-lined plastic basket of hushpuppies they'd usher out as soon as we sat down was my favorite part. I'd always use a butter knife to cut the hushpuppies in half and slather the insides with butter (because being fried in oil wasn't a sufficient amount of fat, apparently). Even though these are savory, my hushpuppies have a hint of sweetness.

---

2 cups (240g) **yellow cornmeal** (fine or medium grind)

½ cup (60g) **all-purpose flour**

3 tablespoons (35g) **granulated sugar**

1 teaspoon **baking powder**

½ teaspoon **baking soda**

1 teaspoon **kosher salt**

1¼ cups (300ml) **buttermilk** (see page 51)

1 large **egg**

2 **scallions**, green tops only, finely chopped

Vegetable oil, for frying

1. In a large bowl, use a whisk or fork to combine the cornmeal, flour, sugar, baking powder, baking soda, and salt.

2. Add the buttermilk and egg to the flour mixture and whisk until combined. Stir in the scallion greens until evenly distributed and then let the batter sit for 10 minutes.

3. Heat 2 inches of oil in a Dutch oven or large heavy-bottomed pot to 375°F. Line a plate with paper towels.

4. Use a spoon to carefully lower a tablespoonful of hushpuppy batter into the hot oil, using a butter knife or small heatproof spatula to coax the batter from the tablespoon into the oil in a single movement. (Be careful—it helps to wear close-fitting long sleeves here, as you don't want the hot oil to splatter and burn your arms.) Fry the hushpuppies in batches, cooking them for about 1 minute per side, then flip them so all sides can become golden brown (some will flip over on their own).

5. Using a frying spider or slotted spoon, transfer the hushpuppies to the paper towel–lined plate. Repeat until all the hushpuppies are cooked. Serve warm.

Lagniappe
(Basic Recipes)

In Louisiana, we have the word *lagniappe,* which means "a little somethin' extra." Bakers are generous by nature. We don't bake entire cakes or dozens of cookies to eat all by ourselves—we do it to share with those we love. That very generosity is why a baker's dozen has one extra (thirteen!) compared with a mathematical dozen. Here's my "little somethin' extra"—a collection of special odds and ends to bring your baking to the next level.

Vanilla Whipped Cream

MAKES 2 CUPS

Homemade whipped cream is infinitely better than the stuff in a can: the texture is creamier, and it's more stable. Homemade whipped cream will hold up in the fridge, retaining its shape. It's also endlessly customizable—the cream can be infused with just about anything, from cinnamon sticks to ground coffee. Just be sure that the cream is extra cold when you're ready to use it—the colder it is, the easier it is to whip up.

If you'd prefer to have unsweetened whipped cream, simply omit the confectioners' sugar.

1 cup (240ml) **heavy cream**

2 tablespoons (15g) **confectioners' sugar**

1 teaspoon **vanilla extract**

Place the cream, confectioners' sugar, and vanilla in the bowl of a stand mixer fitted with the whisk attachment (or in a medium bowl, if using a hand mixer). Whisk or beat on medium speed until you have soft peaks. Then, lower the speed to low, as it's easy to overwhip at this point. Continue beating just until you reach stiff peaks.

storage The whipped cream may be stored in the refrigerator, covered, for up to 3 days.

VARIATION

Peanut Butter Whipped Cream
Add ¼ cup creamy peanut butter to the cream as you whisk it.

Cranberry-Maple Syrup

MAKES 1½ CUPS

Simple maple syrup can be jazzed up by simmering it with fresh fruit and spices. Cranberries are naturally tart, making them a perfect addition. This 10-minute maple syrup mashup is a simple way to add pizzazz to your pancakes or waffles.

1 cup (120g) fresh or frozen **cranberries**

½ cup (160ml) **maple syrup**

¼ teaspoon **ground cinnamon**

1 tablespoon (14g) **unsalted butter**

1 teaspoon **fresh lemon juice**

1. Place the cranberries and maple syrup in a medium saucepan over medium-high heat. Bring to a boil. When the cranberries start to pop, reduce the heat to medium and cook until most of the cranberries have popped and the mixture is thickened, about 10 minutes, stirring often.

2. Stir in the cinnamon, butter, and lemon juice. Serve warm.

storage Refrigerate any leftover syrup in an airtight container for up to 1 week.

Creamy Vanilla Glaze

MAKES ¾ CUP

2 cups (240g) **confectioners' sugar**

3 tablespoons (42g) **unsalted butter,** melted

2 teaspoons **vanilla extract**

3 to 4 tablespoons (45 to 60ml) **whole milk** or **nondairy alternative**

1. Sift the confectioners' sugar into a large bowl.

2. Whisk in the butter, vanilla, and milk until smooth.

Pastry Cream

MAKES 2 CUPS

Pastry cream is one of the fundamental building blocks of pastry, and it's similar to what we think of as custard. It's cooked on a stovetop and requires constant whisking so that the custard doesn't stick to the bottom of the pot and become too hot too quickly (which causes curdling). You may add a tablespoon of liquor or liqueur (such as whiskey or orange liqueur) at the end of step 4 for an extra punch of flavor.

2 large **egg yolks**

1 large **egg**

⅓ cup (40g) **all-purpose flour**

⅔ cup (130g) **granulated sugar**

2 cups (480ml) **whole milk**

1 **vanilla bean,** or 1 teaspoon **vanilla extract**

2 tablespoons (28g) **unsalted butter**

1. Combine the egg yolks, egg, flour, and half of the sugar in a bowl and whisk to combine.

2. Place the milk and the remaining sugar in a medium saucepan. Scrape the seeds from the vanilla into the saucepan and stir. Place over high heat and bring just to a boil, then remove the saucepan from the heat.

3. Whisking constantly, pour half of the hot milk into the bowl to temper the eggs. Then, while whisking, pour the egg mixture into the saucepan.

4. Return the saucepan to the stove and cook over medium heat, whisking constantly, until the mixture starts to boil. Once boiling, continue to cook for 2 additional minutes, whisking vigorously, until thick and smooth.

5. Remove from the heat and stir in the butter. Transfer the pastry cream to a shallow pan and place a piece of plastic flush against the cream to prevent a film from forming. Let cool slightly before refrigerating; make sure the Pastry Cream is thoroughly chilled before using. It can be stored in the fridge up to 3 days.

VARIATIONS

Chocolate

Add 3 ounces melted dark chocolate (55% to 85% cacao) along with the butter once the pastry cream is removed from the heat. Stir to combine.

"Cheat" Pastry Cream

1 (8-ounce) package (1 cup/226g) **full-fat cream cheese,** cold

¾ cup (180ml) **heavy cream**

½ cup (60g) **confectioners' sugar**

1 teaspoon **vanilla extract**

Place all ingredients in a large bowl. Use an electric mixer to beat until very stiff peaks form and the filling smooths out, about 2 minutes. Store covered in the refrigerator until well chilled. The Pastry Cream can be refrigerated up to 3 days.

Lemon Curd

MAKES 2 CUPS

Lemon curd is the perfect balance of tart and sweet, which makes it super versatile. It is great spooned over French toast or used to fill doughnuts. When *The Great American Baking Show* was canceled, I was naturally disappointed. But I didn't want to drown in a puddle of tears, so I made lemon curd out of the lemons, and this solution became my mantra. Indeed, lemon curd is the perfect metaphor for making the most out of a tough situation.

Making lemon curd is meditative. It reminds me of the basic principles of faith and action. It's cooked low and slow, which requires patience and steadiness. You start with lemons, which are sour and too tart to eat on their own. You add something sweet and rich (sugar and eggs), and then you *work*. You've got to constantly whisk. While you're whisking, it may seem like nothing is happening but you've got to have faith and just keep going. Eventually, the eggy liquid transforms into rich, thick, and luxurious lemon curd. That's life—we use what we have and make the most of it. Life is what we bake it.

4 large **eggs**

¾ cup (150g) **granulated sugar**

1 tablespoon grated **lemon zest**

¾ cup (180ml) **fresh lemon juice** (from about 4 lemons)

2 tablespoons (28g) **unsalted butter,** cut into ½-inch pieces

1. Place the eggs, sugar, and lemon zest in a medium saucepan and vigorously whisk until combined. Whisk in the lemon juice.

2. Set the pan over low heat, whisking constantly, until the mixture becomes thick and creamy, about 8 minutes. The lemon curd is ready when it's so thick that it will coat the back of a spoon; if you run your finger across the spoon, the streak will remain visible.

3. Stir in the butter, allowing it to melt into the curd. (If you've slightly overcooked the curd, you can force it through a fine-mesh sieve at this point to remove any curdled bits.)

4. Transfer the curd to a shallow container and place plastic wrap flush on top; this prevents a thick skin from forming. Refrigerate until completely chilled, about 2 hours.

storage Store in the refrigerator in an airtight container for up to 5 days. You can also freeze it for up to 2 months.

VARIATION

Lemon Cream
Increase the butter to ½ cup (113g; 1 stick) for a creamier curd.

RESOURCES

BOB'S RED MILL (BOBSREDMILL.COM)

Nut flours and specialty baking ingredients

BURLAP AND BARREL (BURLAPANDBARREL.COM)

The most fragrant, equitably sourced spices

GUITTARD CHOCOLATE COMPANY (GUITTARD.COM)

American-based artisanal chocolate

KING ARTHUR BAKING COMPANY (SHOP.KINGARTHURBAKING.COM)

Flours and specialty baking ingredients

NORDICWARE (NORDICWARE.COM)

Decorative Bundt pans

SILPLAT (US.SILPAT.COM)

Reusable silicone baking mats

SUR LA TABLE (SURLATABLE.COM)

Bakeware, countertop appliances, and kitchen tools

WILLIAMS SONOMA (WILLIAMS-SONOMA.COM)

Serveware, baking equipment, and kitchen appliances

WILTON (WILTON.COM)

Candy melts, pastry bags and tips, and baking equipment

ACKNOWLEDGMENTS

Mom, six years ago, when I came to you with the idea of starting the @FoodieInNewYork Instagram account, you told me to do it. It felt scary and impossible, but your belief in me sparked this entire journey. And you are still the person I go to every time I want to hear an emphatic "Yes!"

Dad, your steadfast support is invigorating, and your superb storytelling enabled many of these stories to write themselves. Thank you for believing that I'm worthy and deserving of everything good in the world.

To my grandmother, Leona Marcena Clay Johnson: May this book be a testament to your legacy. Your example of sisterhood and dedication to family is my blueprint. Thank you for exhibiting unconditional love.

To my grandmother, Willie Mae Dukes Johnson: Your gentle fortitude and magnanimity showcase your humility. Your green thumb, limitless love, and big heart have made you an impressive shepherd to our family and steward of the land our ancestors entrusted to you.

To my great-great-grandmother and namesake, Lucy Weams Vallery: Thank you for instilling the importance of education and academic achievement in my father. To my grandfather, David Lee Johnson, Sr.: Thank you for instilling that same spirit of excellence in academics in my mother.

Lucy Lomas, I'm so blessed to have a big sister who will fly to London on a moment's notice. You're my biggest cheerleader. Thank you for baking every recipe I publish and for being a superhero mom to my sweet niece and nephew. To my sister Danielle Lomas: Thank you for your support and editing wisdom. To my sister Dawnielle Lomas: Thank you for your emotional support, and compassionate spirit. To my sister Auryona Lomas: Thank you for recipe testing so that I can truthfully say that a thirteen-year-old can make these recipes. To my brother-in-law Evan: Thank you for believing in me. Athena, you are the best cookbook model a girl can ask for. Your insatiable curiosity and love for baking with Auntie Va-Wee warms my heart and encourages me.

Raquel Pelzel, you have championed this book throughout the entire editorial process, and it would not be what it is without your wisdom. Judy Linden, your insight as an agent has made me a more confident author. To my photographer Linda Xiao, food stylist (and sometimes hand model!) Micah Morton, and prop stylist Maeve Sheridan, you ladies are my photo shoot dream team. Thank you for bringing my recipes to life—I felt completely supported. Laura Arnold, Lisa Nicklin, and Catherine Yoo, your recipe testing has made this book immeasurably better. Mia Johnson, Erica Gelbard, Windy Dorrestyn, and the rest of the Clarkson Potter team, thank you for your thoughtfulness and commitment to this project.

Jamila Robinson, your mentorship and friendship make my life richer and easier. Adrian Miller, Kat Kinsman, Julia Turshen, Dana Cowin, and Nancy Hopkins, thank you for your guidance and support. Shauna Ahern, thank you for your editing wisdom. Joy Moeller-Donnell, you are the woman who got the PR ball rolling. Samin Nosrat, your generosity was wholly unexpected and completely changed my trajectory.

Angela Flournoy, thank you for reviewing anything I send your way—from proposal drafts to essays. Laurie Heller, thank you for designing my proposal and recruiting Blake to help with wordsmithing. Roderick Scott, thank you for sharing your publicity expertise. Zoe Zeigler, you're the best roomie, neighbor, and travel bud. Thank you for sharing your marketing insight. Madia Hill Scott, Babara Bridges, Sophia Kapten, Jasmine Ellis, and Casey Sommers—thank you for your steadfast friendship and unwavering support. To my law school besties Nancy Ladner, Jillian Irvin, and Faustina Lee; my Somerville family; SHF; CSO; and Trojan family, your support means the world to me. Thank you. To Diane Evans and Jason Mellad, who invested in my seemingly impossible "foodie" dreams over a decade ago. Karan Lomas and Tayler Davis—I love you and thank you!

Thank you to the Ford Foundation for its incredibly generous support that gave me the space and flexibility to tell this story. To the Kimmel Harding Nelson Center for the Arts, Wildacres Retreat, and Writers' Colony at Dairy Hollow: Thank you for giving me a quiet, peaceful retreat to put words onto paper. Thank you to my Patreon supporters: Lorna Woodside, Mary Miller, Climentene Jones, and Erika Najarian. To the Ginjan Bros: thank you for the warmth of Ginjan Cafe, my Harlem writing refuge. Thank you to every teacher, professor, coach, pastor, and girl scout leader who poured so much into my spirit and who believed in me.

And most important, thank you to all of you, the readers. You cook my recipes and share the love with your friends and family—both in real life and on social media. To my @FoodieInNewYork followers, email subscribers, and fans—you all inspire me beyond measure. This book is for you.

INDEX

Library of Congress Cataloging-in-Publication Data
Names: Lomas, Vallery, author. | Xiao, Linda, photographer.
Title: Life is what you bake it : recipes, stories, and inspiration to
bake your way to the top / Vallery Lomas ; photographer Linda
Xiao.
Identifiers: LCCN 2021004910 (print) | LCCN 2021004911
(ebook) | ISBN 9780593137680 (hardcover) | ISBN 9780593137697
(ebook)
Subjects: LCSH: Baking. | LCGFT: Cookbooks.
Classification: LCC TX763 .L66 2021 (print) | LCC TX763 (ebook)
| DDC 641.81/5—dc23
LC record available at https://lccn.loc.gov/2021004910
LC ebook record available at https://lccn.loc.gov/2021004911

ISBN 978-0-593-13768-0
Ebook ISBN 978-0-593-13769-7

Printed in China

Photographer: Linda Xiao
Editor: Raquel Pelzel
Designer: Mia Johnson
Production editor: Abby Oladipo
Production manager: Jessica Heim
Compositors: Merri Ann Morrell and Zoe Tokushige
Indexer: Elizabeth Parson

10 9 8 7 6 5 4 3 2 1

First Edition